The Basic Elem

Billiards for Beginners

By Steve Mizerak
with Joel Cohen

ICS BOOKS, Inc.
Merrillville, IN

BILLIARDS FOR BEGINNERS. *The Basic Elements of Sports Series*
By Steve Mizerak
Copyright © 1996 Steve Mizerak.,
10 9 8 7 6 5 4 3 2 1
Illustrations Copyright © 1996 by Demetrius Saulsberry

All rights reserved, including the right to reproduce this book or portions thereof in any form or by any means, electronic or mechanical, including photocopying, recording, unless authorization is obtained, in writing, from the publisher. All inquiries should be addressed to ICS Books, Inc., 1370 East 86th Place, Merrillville, IN 46410.

Published by:
ICS Books, Inc.
1370 E. 86th Place
Merrillville, IN 46410
800-541-7323

Library of Congress Cataloging-in-Publication Data

Mizerak, Steve, 1944–
   [Inside pocket billiards]
   Billiards for beginners / by Steve Mizerak w/Joel Cohen.
      p.   cm. — (Basic elements of sports series ; 1)
   Previously published: Inside pocket billiards. Chicago :
Contemporary Books, 1973
   Includes Index.
   ISBN 1-57034-044-7
   1. Billiards   I. Cohen, Joel H.   II. Title.   III. Series.   96-20068
GV891.M69   1996   CIP
794.7'2—dc20

CONTENTS

1 / BEFORE YOU BEGIN **1**
    The Table 1
    Balls 1
    The Cue Stick 2
    Other Cues 3
    Cue Sections 3
    Try Before You Buy 4
    Caring for Your Cue 5
    The Mechanical Bridge 6
    Triangle 7
    Chalk 7
    Powder 8

2 / THE BASICS **9**
    Stance 9
    Bridges 11
    To Shoot Over a Ball 14
    Rail Bridges 14
    Using the Mechanical Bridge 19
    Grip 20
    Aiming at and Sighting the Ball 22
    Stroke 23
    Warmup Stroking 24
    Follow-Through 25
    Special Shots 26
    Follow 26
    Draw 26
    Sticking the Cue Ball 27
    English 27
    Curve 30

3 / PLAYING **31**
    Eight Ball 31
    Playing Strategy/Winning Tips 32
        The Opening Break 32
        Misses 33
        The Best Defense 33
        Position Play 33
        Trouble Balls 36
        Scratching 37
        Spotting 38
        Scratching Deliberately 38
        Runs 38
        Banks and Caroms 39
        Combinations 40

4 / THE GAMES PEOPLE PLAY **41**
    14.1 41
    Basic Pocket Billiards 43
    Fifteen-Ball Pocket Billiards 44
    Rotation 45
    Nine Ball 48
    One Pocket 48

    Golf Pocket Billiards 49
    Cribbage Pocket Billiards 51
    Forty-One Pocket Billiards 52
    One-And-Nine Ball 53

5 / WHAT MAKES A GOOD PLAYER **55**
    Mental Attitude 56
    Confidence 56
    Physical Condition 57
    Dress Comfortably 57
    Psyching 57
    Ambidexterity 58

1
BEFORE YOU BEGIN

First, let's look at the equipment you will use in pocket billiards.

THE TABLE

The standard pocket billiards table is 4 1/2 by 9 feet.

The playing area of the table is known as the *bed* (Figure 1.1). It consists of the cloth-covered slate, the *rails* along the inner edge, off which the balls carom, and the *pockets*. One end of the table, the one from which the cue ball is hit to start the game, is called the *head*. The opposite end is known as the *foot*. About a third of the way from the head of the table, midway between the sides, is a circle known as the *head spot*. An imaginary line through this spot from one side of the table to the other is called the *head string*. Similarly, about a third of the table length from the foot is a circle known as the *foot spot*, and an imaginary line through it is called the *foot string*. In the center of the table is the *center spot*. The imaginary line through the center spot is called—as you may have guessed—the *center string*.

A pocket billiards table has six pockets—one in each of the four corners and one halfway along each side. The size of the pockets may vary considerably.

BALLS

All the balls used in pool games played on full-sized tables are a regulation 2 1/4 inches in diameter and weigh 5 1/2 to 6 ounces. They're all perfectly round and, except for design, are basically the same. The same size balls would also be used on a 5- by 10-foot or 4- by 8-foot table, but you would

Figure 1.1 Overhead view of the pocket billiards table, showing the pockets and spots.

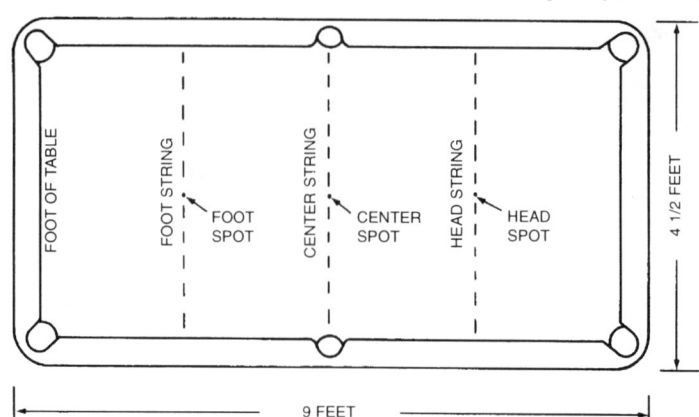

use smaller balls (say, 2 inches) if you play on a smaller table, since the pockets are smaller.

If you play in a billiard room, there's really no advantage to owning your own set of balls. Balls are standardized, and the ones you find in a billiard establishment are usually kept in good condition. Billiard parlors have ball-cleaning machines, but they're expensive to own and really not necessary to have at home. To keep the balls you have at home in good shape, just wash them off occasionally with soap and water and then apply a little plastic polish.

A standard set contains 15 balls, numbered 1 through 15, and an all-white *cue ball*, the ball you hit to propel one or more of the balls into a pocket. Balls 1-8 are solid-colored and balls 9-15 are striped.

THE CUE STICK

The *cue stick* is to a good billiards player what a scalpel is to a surgeon, a drill to a carpenter, or a violin bow to a fiddler. So make sure your cue is well made, properly balanced, and of the right size, and be sure to take care of it.

Even if you play in a billiard parlor rather than on your own table, it pays to own your own cue stick, because you can select one that's comfortable and use the same cue each time you play. Cues have different weights and thicknesses and, to a degree, slightly different shapes, so it's best to buy the one that's best for you.

Early in the history of billiards, cue sticks were shaped like bats and known as "maces." They were clumsy instruments for striking the ball. Through the years they've become lighter and more thinly tapered.

The standard length of a cue stick is 57 inches, but nowadays good players are breaking away from the standard and starting to use sticks that are 58 or even 58 1/2 inches long. You'd be surprised how often that little extra length eliminates the need to use the *mechanical bridge*. You might take a tip from the pros and buy yourself a longer stick. Don't use a stick that's shorter than 57 inches, though, even if you are only 10 years old, or you'll have trouble. Learn with the right equipment.

The circumference of a cue *shaft*, the end of the cue stick with which you hit the ball, varies from 10 to 13 millimeters. The pros use the 13-mm size, and I'd recommend that one to you, especially if you're a beginner, because it provides more hitting surface.

The most important variable of a cue stick is its weight, which you can find stamped in ounces on commercially made cues. There is a tremendous variation in the weights of the sticks. Most professionals use a fairly heavy cue that's between 19 1/2 and 20 1/2 ounces. Some of the pros recommend that you start with a light cue and work up to a heavier cue. But my feeling is that even if you're young, you should start with a regulation weight if you can handle it comfortably.

OTHER CUES

There's a big difference between the cue used for straight pool, which we're concentrating on in this book, and the cues used for snooker and carom billiards. The snooker cue has a very thin shaft and weighs between 13 and 15 ounces. The cushion billiards cue is considerably heavier and gets the ball around the table faster. The straight pool cue is between the other two types in weight.

CUE SECTIONS

Cue sticks have two basic sections—the bottom, or *butt*, and the top, or *shaft*. The stick is tapered from the butt to the leather tip at the end of the shaft, with which you stroke the ball.

A cue stick comes in either one or two pieces. If it's in two pieces, the butt has a metal screw at its top that screws into the bottom of the shaft. Aside from making the stick easier to carry—since you can break it in two parts—there is no particular advantage of a two-piece cue stick over a one-piece, since most cues are basically the same style, with leather tip and white *furl*. You'll find that most billiard parlor cues are in one piece and are unjointed and unwrapped. You can buy a

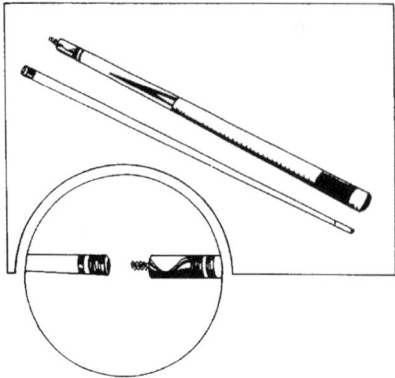

Figure 1.2 THE TWO-PIECE CUE STICK. The bottom half, or butt, of the stick screws into the top half, or shaft.

customized stick in either one or two pieces from any of about twenty custom cuemakers.

I know players who used to carry around one-piece cues to play with in billiard parlors. The one-piece does have some advantages: once it is seasoned, it's not going to warp or bend, and unlike the two-piece, it has no joint that might swell if it gets wet and no fancy wrapping that can be damaged. But you'd look funny if you rode the bus with a cue stick nearly 6 feet long and walked into a pool hall with it. Some players carry extra shafts for their two-piece cues, so that if anything goes wrong they can replace them.

On the butt end of a two-piece there is usually a wrapping of Irish linen, leather, or nylon. Most of the top pros use linen because it does a good job of soaking up sweat left by the hand, thus preventing stickiness.

You'll find that wooden cue sticks are much better than aluminum, since they don't reflect temperature changes as much. Also, if you should accidentally strike your wooden stick on the table, it won't bend in half. It might chip, but it won't bend. In a good cue stick, the shaft will be made of maple or another hardwood, and the butt will be made of ebony or a similar wood.

All cues are basically the same in design, but workmanship can spell a big difference. If you buy from someone who customizes cue sticks, you know that he's going to take his time making yours and that he'll fit the parts together properly. You certainly don't want the screw in a two-piece cue to be off center; if it is, you have problems. And you don't want anything to go wrong with the wrap.

TRY BEFORE YOU BUY

Before you buy a stick or before you select one to play with in a billiard parlor, try out several by taking practice strokes with them. Your cue should be well balanced so that it has its weight evenly distributed and is not butt-heavy. Trying out cues should also tell you which fits you best as to weight and size. But there are other considerations. While you're practice-stroking, look at the tip to make sure it's solid. This is important. The tip should be about 1/8-inch to 1/4-inch high and have a good, rounded shape. The tip's diameter should be 13 millimeters. In three-cushion billiards play, a hard tip is recommended, but for pocket billiards use a medium-hard tip. The wood part of the stick should be free of nicks.

How much should you pay for a cue stick? Well, prices range from about $15 for a one-piece cue to thousands of dollars for a two-piece. I know one man who paid $5,000 for his cue, but that stick had pearls, ivory, diamonds, and everything. The fanciness of your cue isn't going to help your play.

Essentially, the quality of play depends on the player behind the cue stick, no matter whose stick it is. But it helps to have your own cue stick. Jack Nicklaus or Arnold Palmer would play well with my golf clubs or yours, but they'd play better with their own.

Getting back to the price—if you're an average player, you shouldn't pay more than $50 for a two-piece cue. Any cue within the $35 to $200 price range would be a fairly good one that would hold up, but I don't think you should spend more than $200 for your own two-piece cue.

CARING FOR YOUR CUE

It's important not only to buy a proper cue stick but also to take proper care of it.

When you're storing your stick, it's best to use a standard cue rack. If you don't have a rack, stand the stick as flush against the wall as possible. Don't lean the stick against the wall, or you run the risk of putting a bow in the cue.

Wherever you store your cue stick, be sure the temperature isn't extreme or likely to change radically. For example, you should never leave a cue stick in a car overnight. The contrast between the cold of night and the daytime sunshine beating on the stick can do it a lot of permanent damage.

With a two-piece stick, you should always have a case for protection. The harder the case, the better. If you step on or run over a hard case, the stick inside is more likely to escape damage.

When your cue is out of the case, there are several things you can do to keep the stick in tip-top shape. It's a good idea to put some wax on the stick occasionally. I've used a brand name furniture paste wax that really does the job, seasoning the wood and closing up the pores.

The cue should be smooth and clean at all times. For normal cleaning, use a dry rag on the stick every so often. Once in awhile you might want to use a little lighter fluid on a rag to help you close the pores in the wood on your shaft.

A nick in your cue can be very irritating—you'll be aware of it each time you stroke. Many players are tempted to sandpaper their cues to smooth the nick out. Never—*never*—touch the shaft of the cue with sandpaper, because you'll ruin the life of the cue by using the rough foreign element on it. Instead, take the stick back to the person who made it and let him take care of it, if the cue is at all valuable. (I do use grade 600A sandpaper to take dirt or caking off my cue stick, but it's such a fine grade that you can rub your finger with it and hardly feel anything. But you really shouldn't even risk using that.)

THE MECHANICAL BRIDGE

Another piece of equipment sometimes used in pool is the *mechanical bridge*, which helps you make shots that are out of convenient arm's reach. The mechanical bridge has two parts—a stick, which resembles a cue but is generally a foot longer, and a notched metal plate perpendicular to the stick. The notches in the plate are fitted to hold the cue stick, doing the job that your front or *bridge hand* ordinarily would.

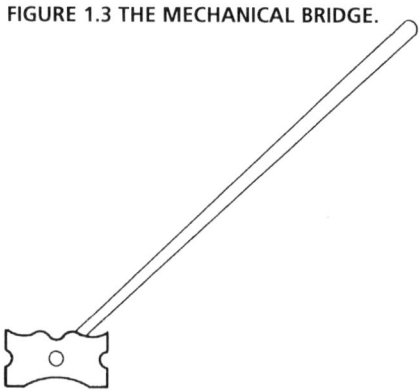

FIGURE 1.3 THE MECHANICAL BRIDGE.

Since most men can stretch farther than most women, the mechanical bridge is sometimes known as ladies' aid. It is also known as a crutch.

Although the mechanical bridge is something you're forced to use on occasion, I don't consider it a desirable tool. The bridge is difficult to control because it leaves you far away from the ball.

If you do have to use it, make sure you lay it down on the table as flat as possible. Avoid the tendency, common to so many players, of lifting the artificial bridge, because then it's likely to move at the metal end and give you a wobbly, inaccurate stroke. As you hold its handle with your normal bridge hand, grip the cue stick at the end and stroke it as if you're throwing a dart, either with an overhand or a sidearm motion.

TRIANGLE

Another accessory is a wooden or plastic triangle, or rack, that enables you to set up the 15 balls in a pyramid shape, apex at the foot spot, for various games of pocket pool.

CHALK

One reason you may sometimes miscue is that your cue comes in contact with the cue ball and there's nothing to grab the tip, so the stick slides off the slippery ball.

Proper chalking will prevent this from happening. The chalk works into the tip and gives it a little bite and grab. Then when the stick makes contact with the ball, it holds its position.

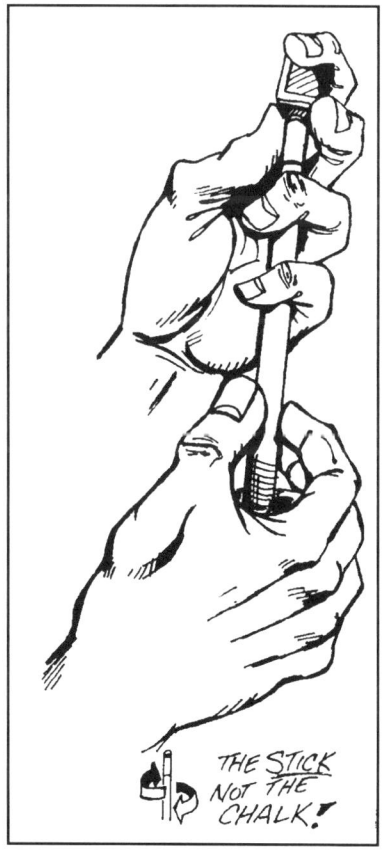

Figure 1.4 CHALKING THE STICK. Hold the chalk on the tip and rotate the stick, not the chalk. Always use a fairly new piece of chalk to avoid getting chalk on the ivory, or furl.

If the tip is smooth and doesn't take chalk, you can improve its grabbing quality by sandpapering it. Use sandpaper on the tip only when necessary. Sandpapering will also keep the tip from flattening out beyond the sides and possibly causing miscues. The leather should be kept even with the cue and slightly rounded on the top.

Another way to rough up the tip is to touch it lightly to a file and roll it. Don't use the file in a scraping movement or it will tear your tip. After you've rolled the tip lightly on a file, wet the sides of the tip with a damp cloth and then polish it with either the back of sandpaper or with a smooth piece of leather. This hardens the sides, insures a firm tip, and prevents the tip from spreading.

When you apply chalk, be sure to do it properly. Don't take the chalk cube in your hand and just rub it back and forth as if you're squeezing orange juice from it, something many players seem to do. The better way is to hold the cube of chalk on the tip of the cue and roll the stick between your palms and fingertips. When you take the chalk cube off, examine the cue tip to make sure you've distributed the chalk evenly. If you've missed a spot, take the edge of the chalk cube and "pencil" in the spots you've missed.

Avoid using a chalk cube that has a deep hole, because it is likely that you'll get the chalk only on the sides of the cue and not on the tip where it is vital. Whenever possible, try to use a newer cube. And try to remember to chalk up after every shot or every other one, so that you don't miscue.

POWDER

If your hands perspire, you'd be wise to apply some powder or resin to them. Don't use too much; just apply a thin coat on your hands so that the cue stick doesn't irritate them as you stroke. Ordinary baby powder is fine for this purpose. In fact, I think it's probably the best thing to use.

2
The Basics

Fundamental to any game played on a pool table are your *stance*, *bridges*, *grip* and *stroke*.

STANCE

The most important thing to remember about your stance is that it has to assure you good balance and allow you freedom of movement for proper stroking. If you're not balanced correctly, your shooting will be erratic. A good thing to do when you've taken your stance is to have someone poke you in the shoulder with his or her index finger. If you lose your balance, you know you're not standing right. Your stance should be firm without being stiff.

Some experts give exact instructions about stance: face the table, stand 10 or 12 inches from it, and place your body in the direction of the shot, with your feet parallel and about as wide apart as your shoulders. Then, they suggest, move your body slightly to the left (if you're right-handed) so that your right arm and shoulder are lined up with the direction of your shot. Turn your right foot about 45 degrees to the right and bring your left foot around so that it remains parallel to the right but is still about 14 inches apart from it.

It's fine to be this mathematical, but not really necessary. I think you should stand the way you feel best. Why hinder yourself by standing in some awkward, cockeyed position? When Don Carter bowled, he held the ball in an unorthodox position, with his wrist twisted and turned in. But how many Don Carters are there? Even when you have to stretch for a shot, it should feel natural.

Figure 2.1 WRONG STANCE. Standing up too straight prevents you from getting a good line of sight on the ball.

Figure 2.2 WRONG STANCE. Bending over too far and your body being too close to the cue stick prevents you from swinging your arm freely.

Figure 2.3 TEST YOUR STANCE...by having someone push your shoulder. If you find yourself losing balance, your stance needs correction.

It all comes back to standing so that you get the most balance. You can't be falling over at the side of the table and still manage to get a smooth stroke with a cue stick. Your feet should be placed in such a way that you can't be knocked over by a strong wind. They should be spread slightly apart, with your weight evenly divided between them. If you're right-handed, hold the cue stick at your right side, with your right hand on the butt and your left hand on the shaft. Face the shot with your left foot forward and slightly turned so that your right arm can swing freely and easily, without interference from your body.

It's usually a good idea to bend your front knee slightly and keep the back knee straight. I don't always do this; it depends on the shot I am making. In normal plays you should keep at least one foot on the ground at all times. In some games, it's a foul if you don't.

Don't stand with your body so far back from the table that you've got no stroke. A common mistake is keeping the butt of your cue stick even with your body. That's wrong. Your body should be closer to the table than the butt of your cue is.

You can judge when you're at a comfortable distance from the cue ball by placing the cue tip almost on the ball, holding your left arm straight, and holding the butt end of the cue in your right hand at your right hip. Once you feel comfortable, bend your body forward, keeping your eye directly over the cue stick.

BRIDGES

A firm *bridge* is vital to a good game of pocket billiards. Your forward hand (the left one, if you're right handed) provides the bridge for your cue stick. There are many different types of bridges. Which one you select will depend on such factors as what you find most comfortable, the closeness of the cue ball to the rail, and whether or not you have to get over another ball to make contact with the cue ball.

A good distance between your bridge hand and the cue ball is 6 to 8 inches but it will depend on the circumstances. Too long a bridge allows the tip to sway and increases the danger of missing the particular point you're aiming at on the cue ball.

The best way to make a bridge (Figure 2.4a-c) is to (a) make a fist, (b) place your knuckles down on the table and (c) lift your thumb to create a crevice where you will rest your cue. From this basic position, you can make all sorts of bridges, from one in which your

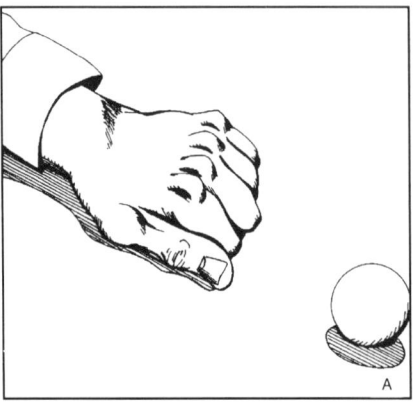
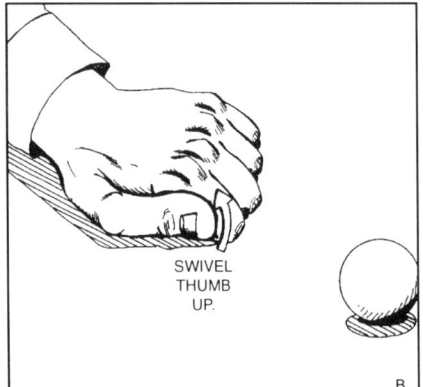
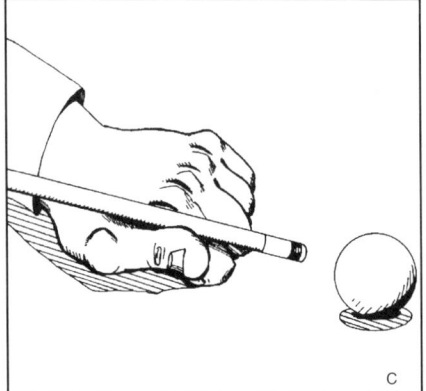

Figure 2.4 A BEGINNING PLAYER...should start making a bridge this way. First, place your fist on the table, with your finger knuckles touching the bed of the table. Raise your thumb and place the cue stick between your thumb and index finger.

fingers lie flat and extended to one in which your hand rises up, balanced on your fingertips.

When you've gained some experience, you might want to start making a bridge this way (Figure 2.5). First (a) place your entire hand on the table, with the heel of your hand firmly on the cloth and your fingers extended, (b) bend your index finger so that the tip of it forms a loop against your thumb, (c) place the cue in the groove between your thumb and index finger, and then through the loop you made with your index finger and thumb. Pull your index finger back firmly against the cue.

Some players recommend that you double under the second joint of your middle finger, which, with your other two fingers spreading and pressing firmly against the table, will form a sturdy support with the heel of your hand and your thumb, which are also on the table. The cue passes through the circle of your index finger, thumb and middle finger (Figure 2.6).

You can hold the cue stick *closed*, with your index finger curled over it to keep the cue from sliding, or *open*, with the cue resting on the crease

The Basics

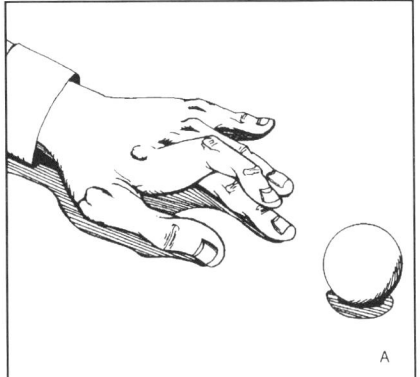

Figure 2.5 AN EXPERIENCED PLAYER...might make a bridge by extending his fingers, raising the thumb and index finger, and placing their pads together. The cue stick fits into the loop made by the thumb and index finger.

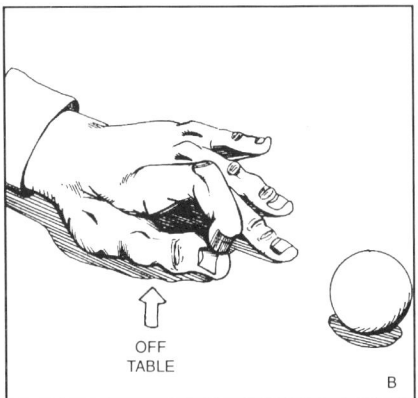

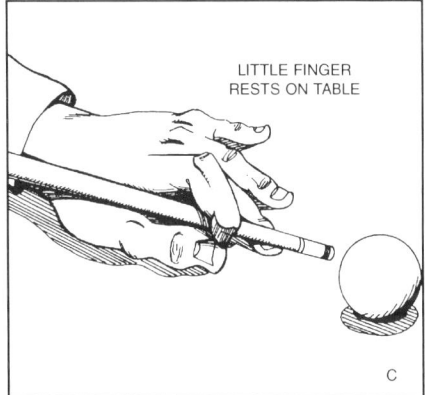

Figure 2.6 THE FLAT OPEN BRIDGE...is for the more advanced player. From the fist you made, open your fingers and, with your palm on the table, raise your fingers slightly so that your hand bends. Elevate your thumb, cradle the cue between your thumb and index finger, and stroke.

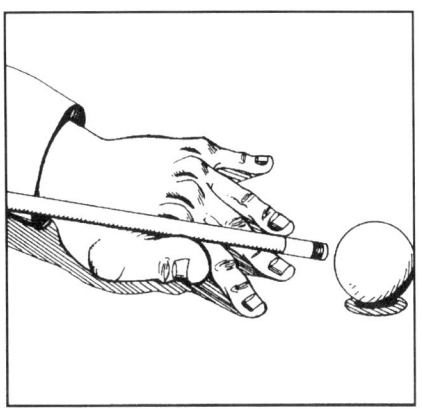

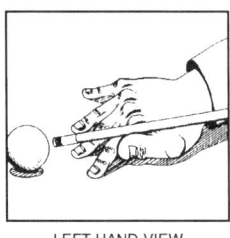

LEFT-HAND VIEW

at the base of your thumb, between your thumb and index finger. The closed grip, with the index finger curled over the cue, is most frequently used because the cue stick can't go anyplace you don't want it to. Professionals tend to use various styles of bridges. You'll find yourself using different ones to meet different situations. For ordinary situations on the table, the open or closed bridges will do equally well.

On a *draw shot*, which we will discuss in detail later, you want the cue ball to come back to you after it hits the object ball. To make this shot, use a closed bridge. For a *follow shot* where you want the cue ball to follow the object ball, an open bridge is generally advisable.

TO SHOOT OVER A BALL

Your bridge hand is the guide to where you're going to hit the cue ball. Therefore, to shoot over a ball and elevate the cue stick, you should raise the wrist and fingers of your bridge hand rather than raise the butt of the cue. Raising the butt is a common temptation that you should avoid if possible. Similarly, when you want to hit the cue ball low, all you usually have to do is lower your bridge.

When you're shooting over a ball, it's a good idea to keep your fingers, from their tips to first joints, on the table, pressing on them hard until you feel solid support. Raise your wrist and palm; then curl your thumb above your index finger and stroke the cue stick between them.

Before you stroke, make sure the bridge is solid. In hitting over an obstructing ball, it's wise to keep your bridge hand as comfortably close to the cue ball as possible, without touching the cue ball with your stick or hand, which constitutes fouling.

RAIL BRIDGES

When the cue ball is close to or touching the rail, you have to use a rail bridge, a type of bridge in which some or all of your fingers and hand and sometimes the cue rest on the rail. In some rail bridges, your index and middle fingers press gently against either side of the cue and form a slot through which the cue slides.

There are several variations of the rail bridge, depending mainly on how close the cue ball is to the rail. If it's within, say, 6 inches of the rail, the four fingers of your bridge hand should be laid across the rail. The cue, which rests on the rail, would then be stroked through the middle and index fingers, with your index finger over the cue and your thumb controlling it from below.

Figure 2.7 THREE RAIL BRIDGES...for use when the cue ball is close to the rail but not frozen to it. In the first picture, the thumb is folded under the palm, and the cue stick travels along the thumb and in between the index and middle fingers. In the middle picture, the thumb and index fingers form a loop through which the cue stick slides. In the bottom picture, the fingers are held on the rail. The cue fits between the thumb and the index finger. This third bridge is an unsteady one that you should try only if you're an experienced player.

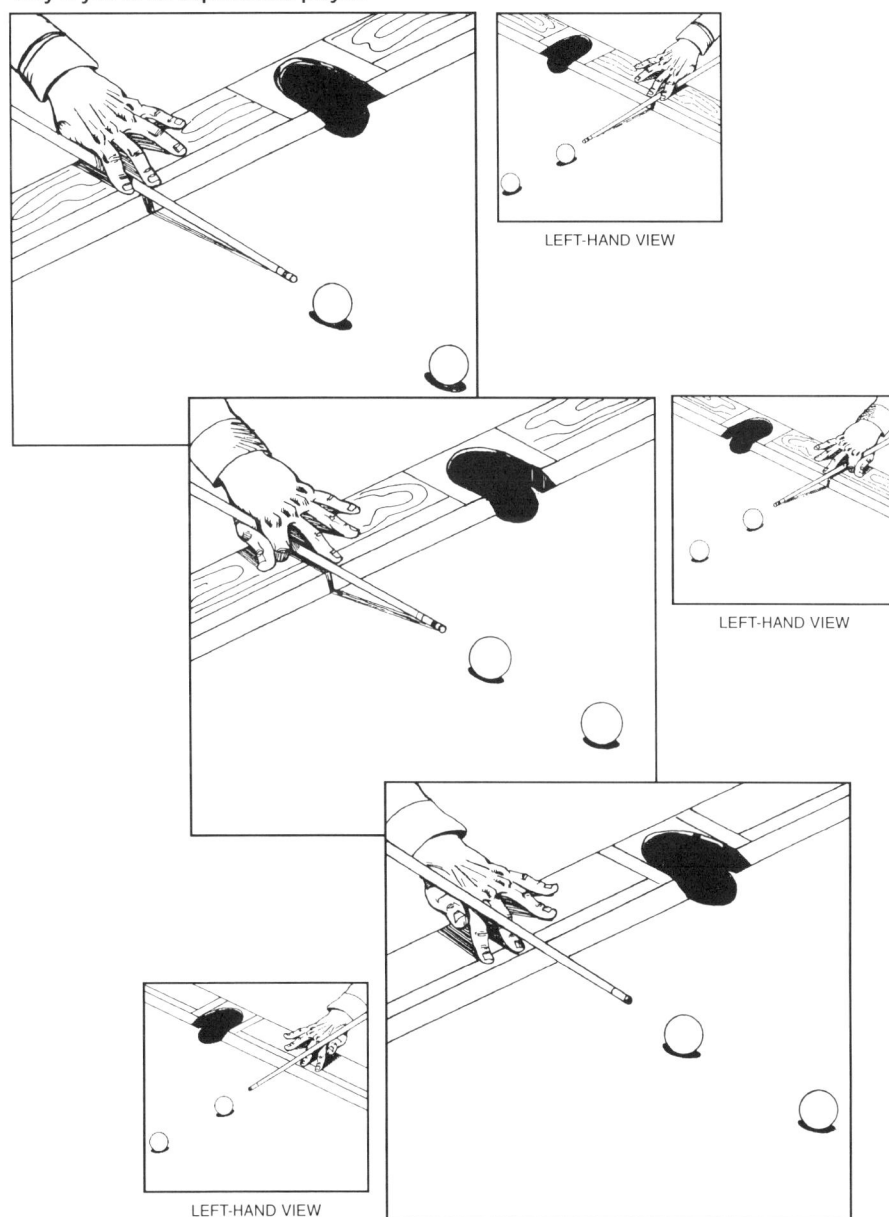

Figure 2.8 WHEN THE CUE BALL IS FROZEN...to the rail, use one of these rail bridges. First picture: Place fingers on the rail, with palm down, and raise your thumb. Cradle the cue stick between the thumb and the index finger. The cue stick should slide along the rail, with the thumb and index fingers as guides. Middle: For more experienced players. Place fingers on the rail; raise palm and press down on the tips and first joints of your fingers. The cue stick rests on the rail as you stroke. It travels between the thumb and curled index finger and then through the index and middle fingers. Third picture: An unsteady bridge for only very experienced players. Place tips and first joints of fingers on rail; bring thumb up and raise wrist; cradle the cue stick between your thumb and index finger.

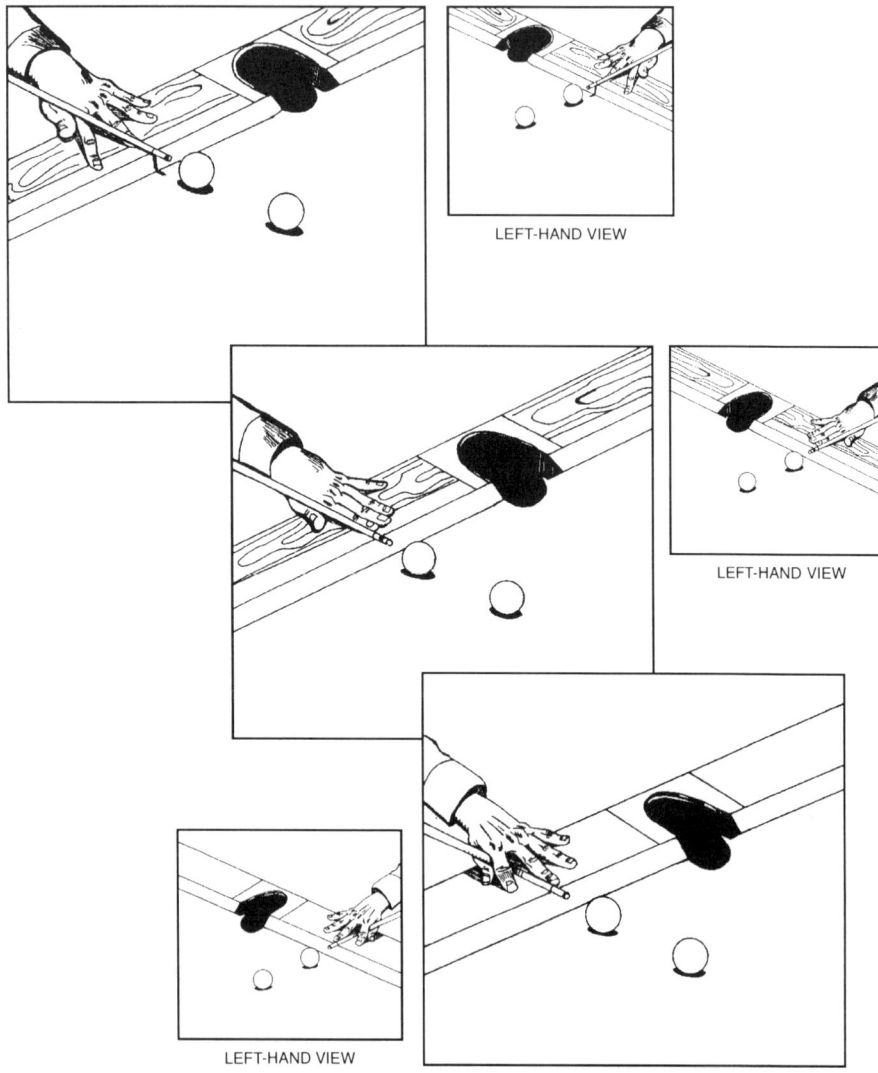

The Basics

If, however, the cue ball is only an inch or two away from the rail, use the same principle but pull your fingers back from the cushion, and let your thumb and index finger give greater control to the cue stick. Do this with your index finger looped around the cue and both your index finger and thumb off the rail. Your thumb should be braced against the outer rail. The cue is stroked along the rail through the loop of the index finger and alongside the middle finger. When the cue ball is right against the rail, or frozen, and your shot roughly parallels the rail, you should rest your thumb, your index finger, and part of the heel of your hand on the rail, while your other fingers position themselves on the bed.

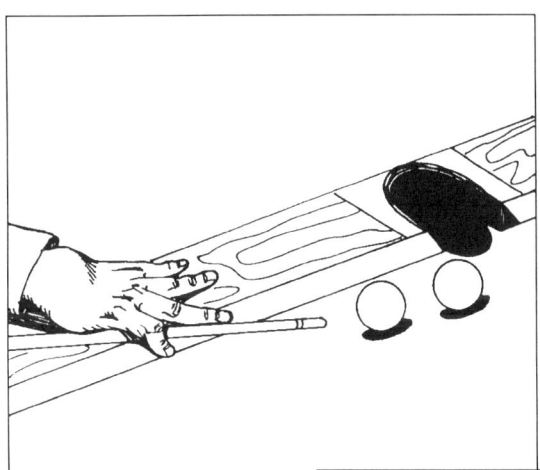

Figure 2.9 STROKING PARALLEL TO THE RAIL...when the ball is against the rail is accomplished by placing the first joints of your middle, ring and little fingers on the rail. Fold your thumb under your upraised hand and loop your index finger over the cue. Slide the cue stick between the index finger and the rail.

Figure 2.10 STROKING AT AN ANGLE TO THE RAIL...when the cue ball is frozen on the rail, fold your thumb under your hand, and stroke, making sure the cue stick is resting on the rail.

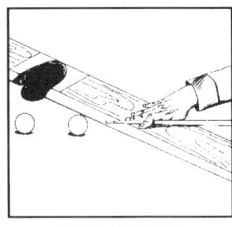

LEFT-HAND VIEW

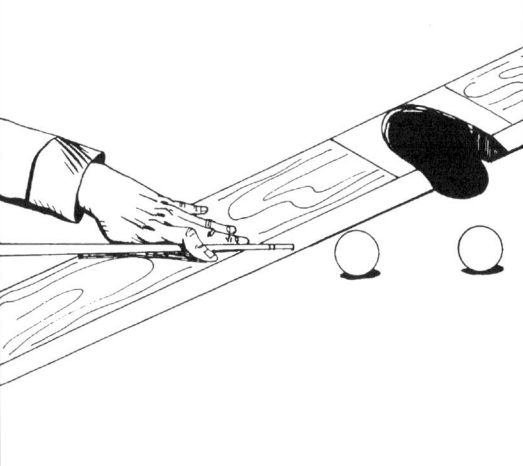

Figure 2.11 THE CUE BALL AND THE OBJECT BALL...are both frozen to the rail. Here are two bridges you can use.

Place your middle, ring, and little fingers on the table. Let your index finger rest on the rail; fold your thumb under your palm. Stroke between your index and middle fingers, making sure the cue is resting on the rail.

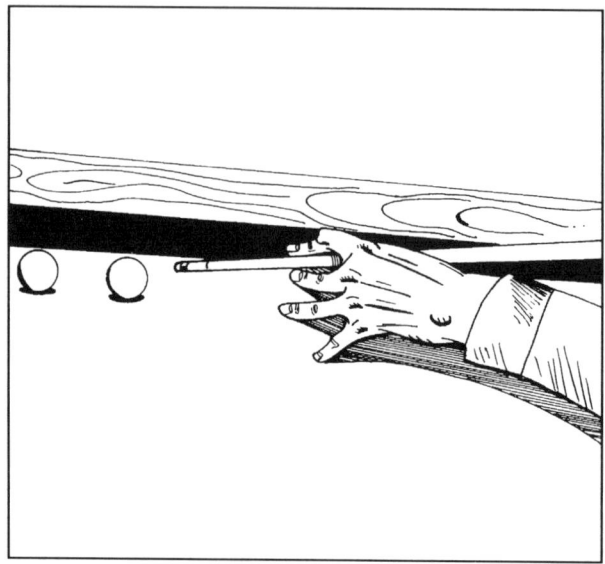

Figure 2.12 Place your fingers on the table. Rest your hand on the rail and raise your thumb. The cue stick rests in the cradle provided by the thumb.

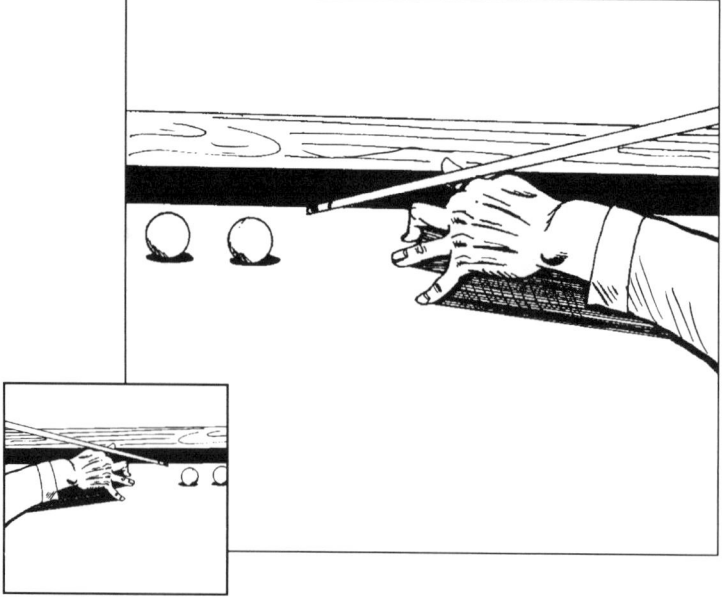

LEFT-HAND VIEW

The Basics

There may be times when the cue ball is more than 6 inches from the rail but not far enough away to let you place your entire bridge hand on the table. In this case, the heel of your bridge hand should be rested on the rail, while your fingers and thumb hold the cue stick in the usual way.

Whatever bridge you use, your bridge hand should grasp or otherwise control the shaft of the cue tightly enough so that the stick won't wobble, but loosely enough so that it moves smoothly when you stroke. If you notice that the forward motion of your stick is being impeded by the skin of the index finger curled over it, you know you're holding the cue too tight. Then, obviously, you should relax your hold a bit. If your stroking is proper, the cue stick shouldn't wobble.

USING THE MECHANICAL BRIDGE

When using the mechanical bridge, remember to keep it as flat as possible on the table. Resist the tendency of many players to raise the bridge, because if you do that, the part of the shaft that is resting on one of the notches of the bridge is going to start moving, spoiling the smoothness and accuracy of your stroke.

To keep the mechanical bridge flat and steady, hold it flat on the table between your middle and index fingers and keep the heel of your hand pressed firmly on top of it. Don't hold it at the very end of the stick.

The bridge should lie to the side of the shot that is away from your power or stroking hand. In other words, if you're right-handed, the artificial bridge should lie to the left of your shot.

FIGURE 2.13 THE RIGHT WAY...to use a mechanical bridge. The bridge hand holds the handle firmly on the table.

Figure 2.14 CORRECT STROKING ACTION...when using the mechanical bridge comes mostly from the wrist. The cue stick is held between the thumb and index finger.

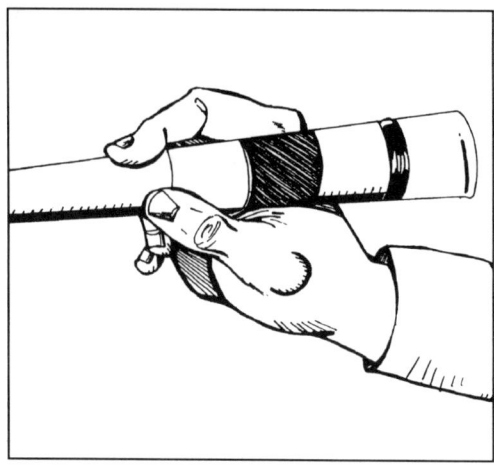

To grip the butt of the cue, use a turned-up version of the usual grip. The cue lies on your thumb with your middle and index fingers on top of the stick.

When using the artificial bridge, sight straight down the cue stick to the cue ball. It's helpful to have the notched head of the bridge a few inches from the cue ball so that you contact the desired point on the cue ball. Which notch or groove you use on the substitute bridge will depend on which spot on the ball you want to hit.

GRIP

The power of your stroke comes from the hand that controls the butt of the cue stick. You should grip the cue stick with your power hand (your right hand, if you're right-handed) about 6 to 8 inches from the butt end. Some players suggest that you hold the cue stick about 4 inches behind the balance of the cue, the point at which the weight of the cue is the same on either side. The butt of the cue should be cradled in the palm of your power hand, with your thumb, index, and middle fingers gripping it firmly and the other two along just for the ride.

Regardless of the situation on the table, you should grip the butt end of the stick in the same fashion. If you find you're doing it differently, there's probably something wrong. You know you're changing your style, and it shouldn't be done.

The Basics   21

Figure 2.15 THE WRONG WAY...to grip the cue stick. Don't leave any space between the cue and the skin between your thumb and forefinger, but don't grip the cue too tightly, either.

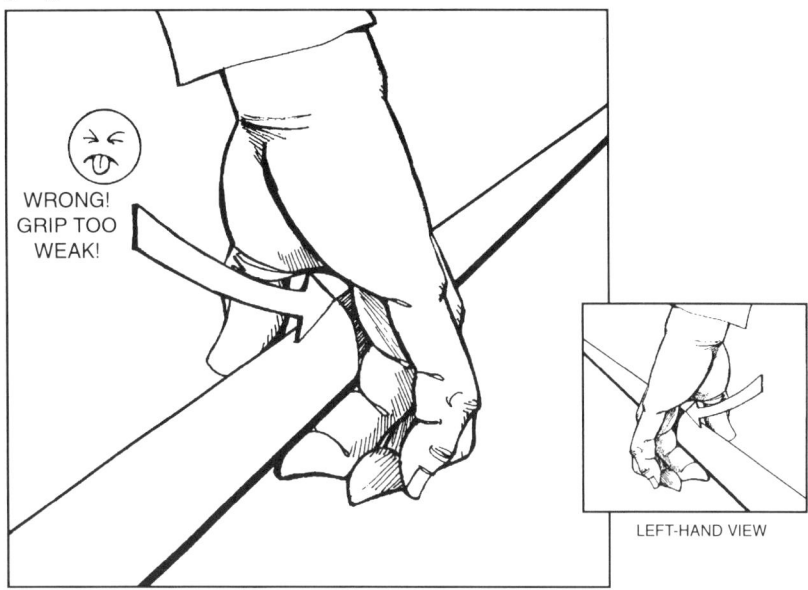

Figure 2.16 THE CUE STICK HELD CORRECTLY. You should keep the pads of the thumb and index finger together, and the cue stick should flow evenly between the two fingers.

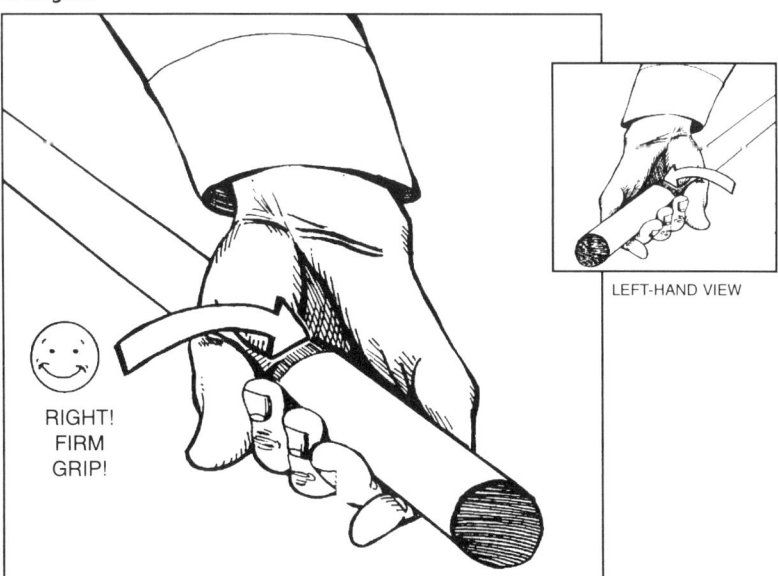

It bears repeating: avoid the mistake a lot of players make—lifting the back hand to elevate the cue. When circumstances force you to elevate your stick—either to get over a ball or to try to hit the cue ball low so that it returns—you should if at all possible raise the bridge hand, not the power or stroking hand.

AIMING AT AND SIGHTING THE BALL

Since a billiard table is unlike a golf course, which rolls and turns, you can depend on the cue ball to roll true and straight after you hit it. There's seldom any need to walk around the table to line up a shot from all angles the way a golfer might do with a putt.

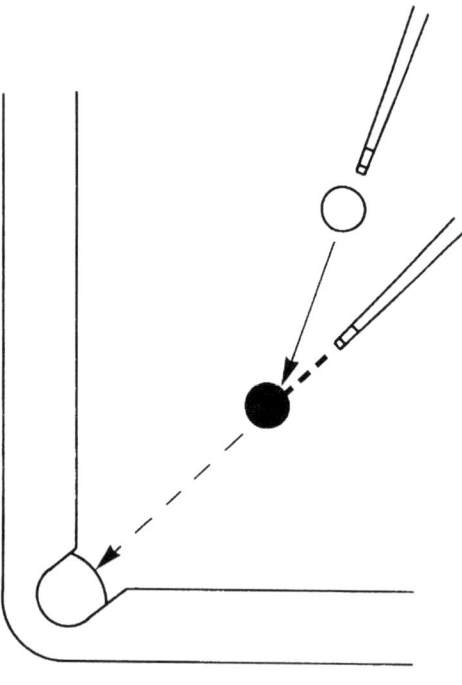

Figure 2.17 Lining up the cue ball with the object ball and pocket. You can use your cue stick to line your object ball up by placing your cue into the center of the pocket through the center of the object ball. The spot where the stick is centered on the cue ball will be the exact spot you should strike the cue.

Measure in your mind the angle at which the cue ball will have to hit the object ball in order to drive it into the pocket, and aim for the point you want to contact. Depending on the situation, there will be times when you want the cue ball to hit the object ball squarely or *full ball*, and other times when you will want it to strike just a portion of the ball or even barely brush it (*thin ball*). Some pros recommend that you imagine a line drawn from the middle of the pocket through the center of the object ball and that you hit the point on the back of that ball where the imaginary line would come through. However you arrive at your point of aim, remember: finding the spot isn't difficult; hitting it is.

The ability to judge which shot you can make and which shot you should take will develop with experience. In straight pool, you should be reasonably sure that you can pocket a ball before calling it. The shrewd player leaves the impossible balls for his opponent.

It's hard to tell you for sure where you should sight first. Probably you'll be looking at the object ball and the pocket simultaneously just before you shoot. Once you've placed your bridge hand on the table and set it in place, it shouldn't move, and your line of aim between cue stick and cue ball should be fixed, so that you don't have to resight as you stroke. You can close one eye when you're sighting, but you need both eyes open when you're shooting.

STROKE

A key point to remember in stroking the ball is that your arm should move only from the elbow down. It should swing like the pendulum of a grandfather clock—back and forth in a straight plane. Your elbow may move just a hair, but if you lift it you'll be raising the cue stick and your stroke will be uneven. Don't move your shoulder either, or you'll be in trouble.

Just keep practicing that pendulum movement until you can feel that you're doing it right. Actually, you can probably see your arm moving, and if you're doing it the right way, you'll be able to tell.

Much of the success of your stroke depends on the wrist action of your power hand. The wrist doesn't act independently; it acts with your lower arm. The snap of your wrist should be coordinated with the pendulum swing of your lower arm. As you swing your arm forward, your wrist should whip the cue stick into solid contact with the cue ball. Remember not to grasp the butt of the cue stick too tightly. The wrist should be loose, not stiff. If you tighten up the wrist, you won't get as good a stroking action as you will if your wrist is flexible.

Most of your stroking action should be wrist action. You need a good wrist, well coordinated with your power arm.

As in hitting a baseball, you need a back swing before striking a cue ball. Bring your cue stick back a distance equal to the length of your bridge and let fly with a quick, level shot.

A good exercise is to place the cue ball about 18 inches from the head of the table and in a direct line with the middle diamonds at the foot and head of the table. Aim at the middle diamond at the foot of the table and try to make the ball return in the same line and hit the end of the cue, which you left in follow-through position. This can be done only if you strike exactly in a vertical line through the ball's center.

WARMUP STROKING

No matter what the situation, you should take several practice strokes before you actually make contact with the cue ball. A golfer takes practice strokes before he or she putts, and a pitcher will go into a winding motion before he or she rears back and throws. A pool player has to rear back and fire too, and you want to make sure your aim and stroke are on the beam.

Some players get up there and—boom!—hit the ball on the first stroke. But you shouldn't. You have to be very conscious of what you're doing. You have to make sure your arm is moving only from the elbow down; you have to make sure your aim is proper. Take your time and stroke the cue three or four times before you take the shot. Too many warm up strokes will tend to make you tired, and too few strokes won't allow you sufficient concentration to properly sight the ball.

Your practice strokes should be deliberate, not jerky. After all, you want the warmup strokes to be the same as your actual shot—except, of course, that in your practice strokes you don't make contact with the ball.

Don't vary your preliminary stroking. It's tempting to do one warmup stroke before an easy shot and five before a tough one. You should take the same number of strokes before every shot, regardless of how easy or difficult the shot appears to be. I've seen hangers—where the object ball is "hanging" right near the pocket—missed by the best of players. It usually happens because they rush into the shot. I've done it myself several times. Once in Chicago I was playing in a tournament and had a shot that was so simple a baby could have made it. The shot was worth a couple of thousand dollars in prize money. I just got up and hit it. The ball ricocheted back and forth from one side of the pocket to the other, and then hung right there on the lip of the pocket. Luckily for me, the cue ball caromed off the rail and put my opponent behind a cluster of balls where he didn't have a clear shot at the ball hanging on the lip. He banked the cue ball but missed the object ball completely. So it was my turn again. Needless to say, this time around I took all the time in the world. I went to the table, went back, put powder on my hands, took a drink of soda, got a towel, wiped my brow, and finally went back to the table and—after some warmup strokes—made my shot. I won the match, but I almost had heart failure because of my hasty carelessness. It taught me a lesson I'll never forget: take practice strokes, no matter how easy the shot. Hangers are missed sometimes.

But they shouldn't be, and wouldn't be if players took some preliminary strokes to get in the groove.

Whether you play a deliberate or a speedy game, take those warmup strokes. Your final stroke will be faster than your warmup as a result of the quick snap of your wrist.

Each player has his or her own pace. I play pretty quickly; I'm not deliberate.

The speed with which you stroke will determine the action of the cue ball, not only before it hits but also after it makes contact with an object ball or cushion. The speed of your stroke should be uniform throughout the game, no matter what kind of shot you're taking.

The intensity of your stroke is another matter. If you just want to nudge the object ball into the pocket, or if you want the cue ball to hit only one cushion, you will naturally hit it a lot more gently than if you want the cue ball to carom off nine cushions.

In any situation, you've got to hit the ball as if you mean it. Hit with some authority—with speed and solidity. You can't baby a ball, or your cue stick will probably swivel and your stroke will be soft and ineffectual. On the other hand, you don't want to hit the ball so hard that you lose control.

How much force an object ball receives is determined by the point of impact with the cue ball and the speed of the stroke.

Exactly how hard you will want to hit the cue ball will depend on your touch and on the feel and judgement you develop with practice. Keep practicing grooving your swing—coordinating your wrist and arm action.

FOLLOW-THROUGH

As in any other sport, the follow-through in billiards is very important. You don't want to start looking up or lifting your cue stick before you've hit the ball solidly. To prevent your stick from striking the cue ball at a spot higher, lower, or more to the side than you want, follow through with your stroke. Stay down in position and keep your cue stick on the table as long as reasonably possible after the shot. That includes keeping your bridge hand in position, too. Otherwise you're likely to twist your body and ruin the accuracy of your shot.

Finish your stroke with the cue a few inches past where the cue ball rested. Don't let your cue tip waver around in the air after you deliver your stroke.

Figure 2.18 HITTING THE BALL DEAD CENTER...is essential when you first start playing pool. Most of your shots will be hit this way.

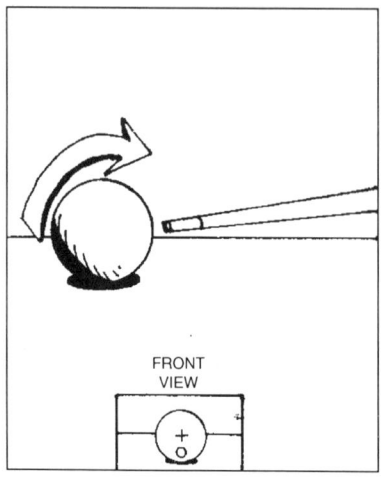

Figure 2.19 FOLLOW. To make a cue ball follow the object ball after it makes contact, hit the cue ball above center.

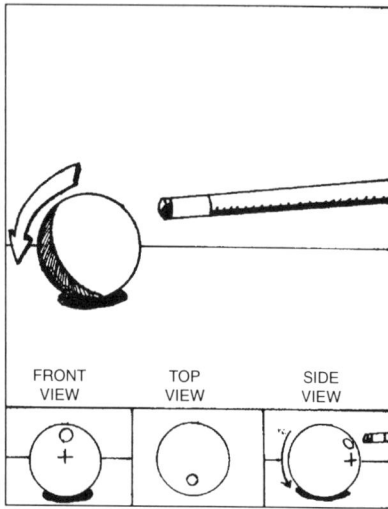

SPECIAL SHOTS

Most of the time you'll want to hit the cue ball in the center. There's less chance of your cue tip slipping off, and a ball struck in the center rolls truer. But under special circumstances, because you want your cue ball to react in a particular way, you'll deliberately hit the cue off-center. These off-center shots have different names and purposes: *follow*, *draw*, and *English*.

FOLLOW

If you want the cue ball to move forward after it strikes the object ball, you should hit it above center with a level cue and follow-through. This shot is called a follow because the cue ball will spring forward in the direction of the object ball. Never hit the cue ball at the extreme top, because there's too much risk of miscuing. Try to keep your bridge hand at a point that enables you to keep your cue level. Hitting the ball too high also spoils accuracy and desired action of your shot.

DRAW

A *draw shot* is used when you want to "draw" the cue ball back toward you after it makes contact with the object ball. You make a draw shot by hitting the cue ball below center with your cue level and then following though. The lower you hit the ball, the more draw you're likely to get, although other factors—how hard you hit and how fast— will also affect the amount of draw. Don't hit it at the extreme bottom. And no matter what type of shot you're hitting—draw or follow— follow straight through.

Hitting the cue ball hard, fast, and low will result in the greatest amount of draw. There may be times when it is necessary to elevate the butt of your cue to draw a shot successfully—for example, if the cue ball is near the rail or if you have to stroke over an object ball. When lifting the butt is necessary, picture the horizontal axis of the cue ball as being at the same angle as the elevation of your cue, and strike the ball below the axis. Otherwise, just hit the cue ball below center, with the stick as level as possible.

STICKING THE CUE BALL

It's possible to hit the cue ball in such a way that it stops dead in its tracks after it hits the object ball. This stop action is sometimes known as *sticking* the cue ball.

Sticking is a difficult trick to accomplish on a table with a new cloth, but usually all it takes is a stroke a little below the center of the cue ball (not as low or as hard as you'd stroke to "draw"). How far below center you should hit it will depend on how far away you are from the ball. When you're close to the ball you don't have to hit it quite as much below center. But be sure to hit the ball only at a normal rate of speed. Excess speed will make the ball draw back; you want it to stick.

ENGLISH

English is a spinning motion created by hitting the cue ball to the left or right of center. The motion affects not only the cue ball when it comes into contact with an object ball or cushion, but also the course of the object ball, which will spin in the direction opposite that of the cue ball.

If you hit the cue ball left of center, the cue ball will spin to the right and curve to the left. This is called left-hand English. The opposite is called right-hand English.

Figure 2.20 RIGHT-HAND ENGLISH. The ball will spin to the left and then curve to the right.

Figure 2.21 LEFT-HAND ENGLISH. The ball will spin to the right and then curve to the left.

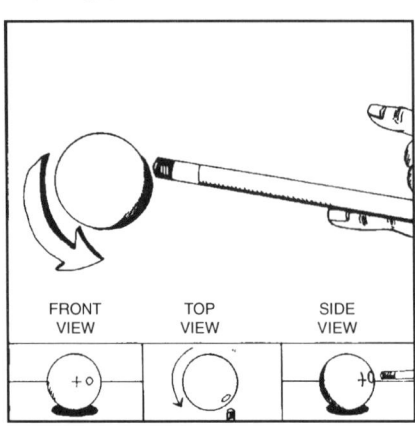
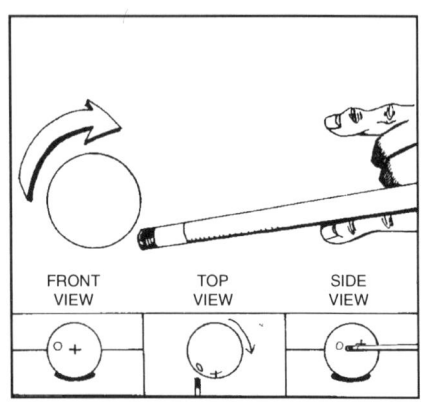

If you're ever going to be an accomplished pool player, English is something you'll have to master. But you can get into more trouble applying English improperly than if you don't use it at all. So use as little English as possible. When you do use it, your stroke can't be rigid; it's got to be sharp and springy. You have to follow through. And you have to allow for the curved path a ball takes when English has been applied.

According to most experts, you can apply English on 99 percent of all billiard shots by striking the cue ball only the width of a cue tip from the center of the ball. Going wider than that point to either side increases the chances of miscuing.

There are two basic kinds of English—*natural* and *reverse*. Natural English, sometimes called running English, is applied to the side of the cue ball toward which you want it to travel after it hits the object ball or cushion. In other words, a cue ball hit to the left of center will travel left after it hits a ball or cushion.

Reverse English is applied to the side of the cue ball that is opposite the direction you want it to travel after it hits an object ball or a cushion.

Natural English adds speed to the cue ball after it hits a cushion and widens the angle of the ball caroming off the cushion.

Reverse English does the opposite. It slows the ball's speed, narrows the angle, and actually reverses the course the cue ball would normally travel after striking a cushion.

Figure 2.22 THE TYPES OF ENGLISH. The top drawing shows the difference between reverse and natural English. The bottom drawing shows where the ball travels when left-hand and right-hand English are used.

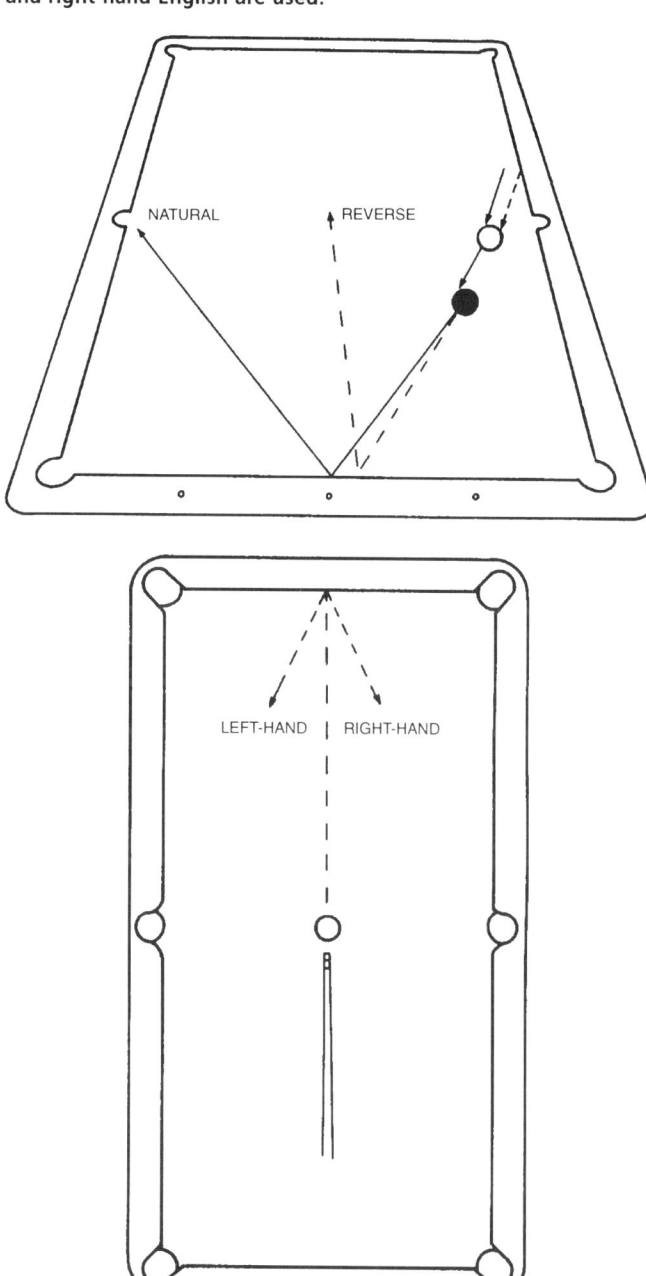

CURVE

As mentioned above, if you apply natural English to the cue ball on the right, it will spin counterclockwise (left) but curve to the right. The longer the shot, the wider will be the arc of this curve. When you're planning your shot, you must take into account what the path of that curve is likely to be.

For example, on a table-length shot, if you want to barely touch the object ball on its left side, a left-English shot might curve too much and miss the object ball. So you would estimate the curve and compensate by aiming to hit more of the object ball. In other words, you have to allow for the amount of curve the cue ball will take and hit it according to the degree of cut you want the object ball to have.

There are different degrees of English you can create. The more spin you want, the harder you hit the ball.

At times you'll want to combine English with either draw or follow. In any event, you should devote a good deal of practice to perfecting each one of these techniques, for how well you master them will determine how well you play position—the mark of a good pocket billiards player.

Figure 2.23 A PRACTICE DRILL...for position play consists of putting all the balls in a circle and placing the cue ball inside the circle. You should try to pocket all the balls while making sure that the cue ball touches only specific object balls and does not touch the rail.

3
Playing

EIGHT BALL

You've heard the expression, "behind the eight ball." This is the game it comes from. In *eight ball*, you must try as hard not to do anything to lose the game as you try to do things to win it.

Object
The object of eight ball is to pocket a specific seven of the 15 object balls and then pocket the 8-ball before your opponent sinks his or her seven object balls and the 8-ball.

One player or side has to pocket the balls numbered 1 to 7; the other, the balls 9 to 15. The 8-ball must be saved for last.

The game is played with a cue ball and 15 object balls, which are racked at the foot spot, with the 8-ball in the center of the triangle.

The Break
If you break, you don't have to call any shots. If you pocket one or more balls on the break you have your choice of making the 1-7 balls or the 9-15 group your objects. If you don't pocket a ball on the break, your opponent gets the choice, and you take the other category.

Rules
The player gets credit for all balls legally pocketed—except balls that are in the opponent's group. If you pocket a ball belonging to your competitor, he or she gets credit for it. If you pocket only one of your opponent's balls and none of your own, it's a miss and your turn ends.

After all the balls in your group have been pocketed, you may go after the 8-ball. Although you didn't have to call the other shots, you must call this one.

If you're shooting directly at the 8-ball without banking, you must either pocket the ball or make it or the cue ball contact a cushion after striking the 8-ball. If you fail to do either of these, you lose the game!

If you pocket the 8-ball on the opening break, you lose the game. If you accidentally pocket the 8-ball before you pocket all the balls in your numerical group, you lose the game. If you're banking the 8-ball, you must hit the 8-ball or you lose the game.

When you're playing for the 8-ball, you must hit that ball first. If you pocket it on a combination, you lose the game.

Remember, you've got to call the pocket where you intend to drop the 8-ball. If it goes into a pocket you didn't designate, you lose the game.

When you're shooting to make the 8-ball, you lose the game if the cue ball scratches in a pocket.

PLAYING STRATEGY/WINNING TIPS

The Opening Break

One of the most important shots of any game played on a pool table is the opening break, the shot in which the racked-up balls are broken apart at the beginning of the game. The shot can make or break your game.

Try to make your set of balls without breaking up clusters or any type of trouble balls that might be an advantage to your opponent.

In baseball, the other team always gets a chance at bat. In tennis, your opponent always has a shot at returning your serve. But billiard games are one form of competition in which one player can win without allowing his opponent a turn. So you can see why the break is so important.

If you are the player to break in the game of *one pocket*, where you're trying to put all the balls near your pocket, or in *nine ball*, where you might make the winning ball on the break, or in *rotation*, where you're trying to pocket a ball, it would definitely be to your advantage. But in 14.1, where the chance of making a called shot on the break is so slim and the likelihood of setting up easy shots for your opponent is so great, it is definitely *not* to your advantage to break.

To decide who breaks, you and your opponent can flip a coin, choose, or do what the pros do–*lag*. To lag, you each take a turn shooting the cue ball down the side rail to the foot rail, trying to bring it as close back to the head rail as possible. The player who comes closest to the head rail has the option of whether or not to break. Remember: if you win the toss or lag, you can request your opponent to break.

The particular game and your game strategy will determine where to place your cue ball, the force with which you hit the cue ball, the spot on the cue ball at which to aim your cue stick, and the section of the rack of balls at which you aim.

If you are the one who has to break, remember that a good break will leave your opponent with either no shot or with a tough one.

If you're lucky, you won't leave your opponent with any decent shot. When it's your turn again, if you have a choice between hitting a close shot and a distant one, take the one that's nearer. It's almost always the easier shot.

The player who opens doesn't usually call a ball and a pocket because the chances of making the shot are so unlikely.

Misses

A missed shot is an error that ends your turn. There's no penalty if you fail to make the cue ball contact the designated object ball, provided that the cue ball hits at least one other ball and drives it into a cushion, or a pocket, or the cue ball hits a cushion after hitting the object ball.

Object balls that are pocketed illegally are spotted on the foot spot. If that spot is occupied, the ball is put directly behind it on the (imaginary) *long string*, that runs the length of the table, through the head spot and foot spot. If you are playing in a tavern or on a coin-operated table, a missed shot simply means that it is your opponent's turn.

The Best Defense

The best defense in pocket billiards is a good offense, primarily because of the peculiar nature of the game—the fact that one player can win without his or her opponent ever getting a shot. I've won and lost games in which this has happened.

This is not to say that you never play defensively. There are times when you should play a safety, a shot that you deliberately take to leave the ball safe, or tough for your opponent, with no attempt or intention of making a point. In other words, you more or less sacrifice your turn and leave your opponent with what you hope is an impossible shot. You would do this when you're in a very tough situation, when you don't have a shot that you can make, or when you lack the confidence that you can make any shot open to you. Most of the time you want to be careful that you don't scratch.

Position Play

No matter what your playing level, you should always take the shot you think you can make. If you're a beginning player, always take the easiest shot first. Do your light work before you take on the heavy tasks, and don't overly concern yourself with position. As you develop your skills, however, you should think more about position and making the shots that will follow the one you're attempting now.

All that position involves is planning ahead, trying to pick your next shot or shots. When all 15 balls are on the table, look only one or two shots ahead. But when you get down to, say, five balls, you should decide the order in which you intend to play all five and position your cue ball on each shot accordingly.

On break shots, or when you are trying to break up a cluster of balls, you can't play position because you don't know what's going to happen. Here's where the element of luck plays a big part. Once you've scattered the balls, you can try position play.

The key thing to remember is that in position play you're trying not only to pocket your object ball, but also to have your cue ball located in such a position after the shot that you have clear sailing to make the next object ball.

To improve your position play, practice these two exercises:

1. Line up the balls in a circle in the middle of the table, with the cue ball in the center. Try to make every single ball without missing and without letting the cue ball touch the rail. If it hits the rail, you've lost. To do this exercise, you're going to have to call all your billiard skills into play: draw, follow, and English.

2. Place a ball at the foot spot and form a large "L" with all the other balls. Then, with the cue ball anywhere outside the "L," try to pocket all the balls in the corner pocket, starting with the ball closest to the rail.

To help yourself when you play, try to hit the smallest number of balls possible on one shot.

When you scatter a cluster of balls, don't scatter them too hard. You want all the balls within the same half of the table. You should try to play in the four pockets that are at the middle and foot of the table rather than in all six pockets, because you don't want to have to be shooting your cue ball up and down the table. Imagine a line across the middle spot and do your best to work from there to the foot. If any balls go up to the other end, try to pick them off as soon as possible. Figures 3.1, 2, 3, 4 and 5 show how I would approach some common pool situations. Study these diagrams to get some idea of how to play position.

Playing 35

Figure 3.1 Stroke the cue ball to the right of center, so that it will carom off the rail and be in position for the next shot.

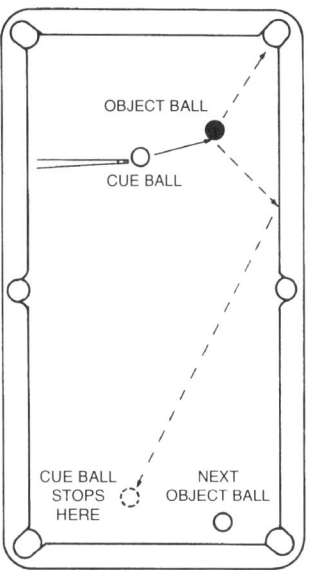

Figure 3.2 Hit the cue ball to the left of center, so that it will carom off the rail and be in position for the next shot.

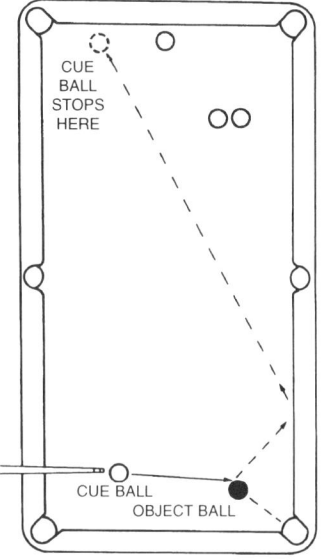

Figure 3.3 To be in position for the next shot, the cue ball must follow the object ball.

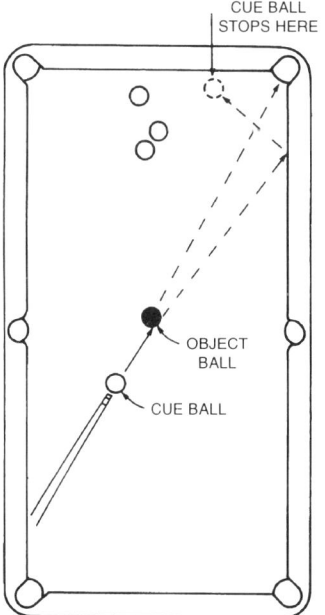

Figure 3.4 To be in position for the next shot, the cue ball must come back toward you after it hits the object ball. Make a draw shot by striking the cue ball below center.

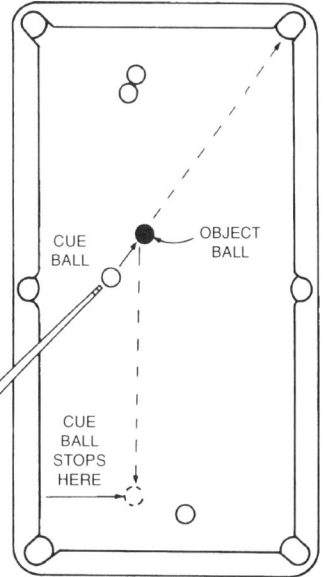

Figure 3.5 In this situation, use a combination of follow and left-hand English.

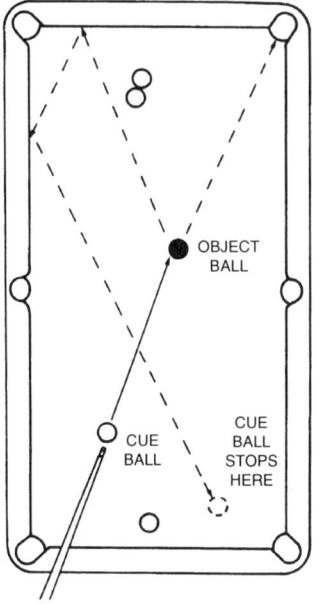

Figure 3.6 In this situation, I would pocket the object ball and have the cue ball carom off the lower rail and break up the cluster of three balls.

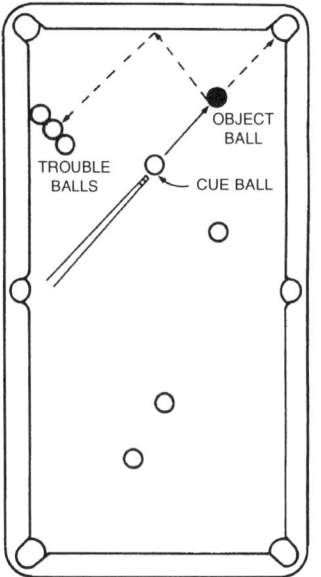

Trouble Balls

No matter how well-planned your strategy may be, you'll occasionally be confronted with *trouble balls,* balls clustered together near a rail, away from the rack at the foot of the table, or in some other location in such a way that they loom as trouble. Try to clear these off first. Even if you have to alter your game plan, break up those trouble balls, or later in the game they'll give you exactly that. (Figures 3.6 and 7).

Because you want to avoid unforeseen problems, as you gain experience you will usually try to avoid having your cue ball graze

Figure 3.7 In this situation, I would pocket the object ball in the side pocket. I'd do this by using English and hitting the ball on its left side. The cue ball should carom off the side rail and break up the cluster of balls lying on the foot rail.

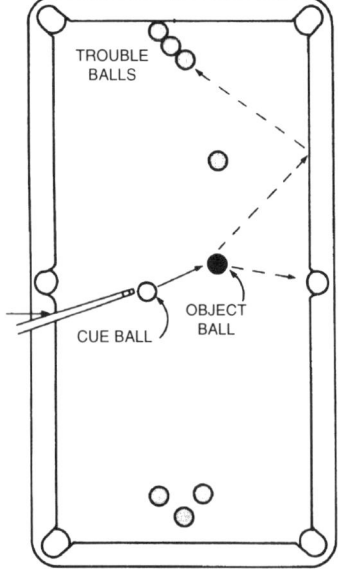

any ball other than the one you're trying to pocket. The ball you graze is liable to come into the path of your next shot and destroy your strategy. Also, you have little idea of where the cue ball will go if it should accidentally graze another ball.

In dealing with trouble balls you must try to control that ever-present element of luck. You want to be able to just go "bing" and pocket your object ball according to plan. You don't want to take a chance on what your next shot is going to be. So get rid of those trouble balls as soon as possible and leave yourself clear for execution of your game plan.

Scratching

A *scratch* is a miss or a shot that usually results in a penalty. It occurs in several different ways.

If you hit the cue ball into a pocket in eight ball, a ball of yours is taken out and placed on the foot spot. If the cue ball follows your object ball into the pocket, both balls are respotted—the object balls at the foot spot or right behind a ball that is already there, the cue ball anywhere behind the head string.

If the cue ball jumps off the table, it's a scratch. In championship play, the same rules apply to an object ball that goes off the table. In games other than championships, an object ball that jumped off the table would be spotted at the foot string. Your inning or turn would end, as it does with any scratch.

Failure of your cue ball and four other balls to hit a rail on the opening break in eight ball games is also a scratch, as noted. You also scratch anytime your cue ball fails to hit another ball, or if both your cue ball and an object ball fail to hit a rail (unless a ball is pocketed).

Rules relating to scratching vary with the particular game. In nine ball, for instance, a scratch brings only the end of your shot, while in 14.1 or any other straight pool game, it's both a one-point penalty and the end of your inning.

There are several ways of preventing your cue ball from following an object ball into the pocket, even on an easy straight-in shot. A draw shot, hitting the cue ball below center to make the cue ball stop, is one way. But even if you hit the cue ball dead center, it shouldn't go in. You can prevent the cue ball from going into the pocket by not hitting it very hard and by hitting it so that it glances off the object ball at a slight angle.

If your cue ball is lined up straight with the pocket, hit the object ball a little to one side, so that the cue doesn't follow it in. If you want to hit the object ball in the middle, make sure that you hit the cue ball low to bring it back (draw).

If the object ball is at an angle, rather than lined up straight between your cue ball and the pocket, use your judgement and hit the cue ball off to the side that's away from the pocket.

How hard you should strike the cue ball will depend on how far away you are from the object ball and whether or not you're playing position.

Spotting

When you have cue ball in hand and there are object balls in the head string, place the object ball that's nearest to the string on the foot spot. You do the same thing when the 8-ball is the object ball and is lying within the head string and you've got the cue ball in hand.

Scratching Deliberately

As you develop your playing skills, there will be times when you'll want to scratch deliberately rather than risk setting up your opponent a long run on an open table. This is part of defense play, which figures so importantly in pocket billiards.

The same might apply whenever you're confronted with a tough situation—when you don't have a shot you can make or when there is a shot, but you don't have confidence that you can make it. In that case you should figure, "Why do the job for my opponent?" Let your opponent break the cluster of balls open.

Actually, I don't recommend this outside of championship play. If I were you, I would never take more than one or two scratches in a row.

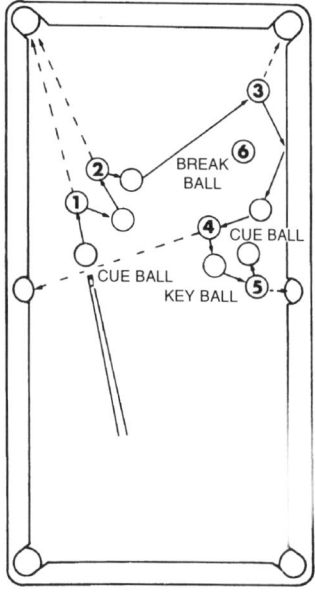

Figure 3.8 When you pocket ball 1, draw the cue ball back to the right. Pocket ball 2 and use a stop position. Pocket the third ball and draw the cue ball along the rail so that the fourth ball can be pocketed. Use the stop position and then pocket the fifth ball.

Runs

The ability to deal with the break shot is more important than being able to get on a high run. You can't manage a high run without being able to make the break shot.

High runs are interesting to fans—and to players, of course, since prizes are sometimes given for them. Willie Mosconi once pocketed 526 balls in a row in an exhibition. But you can win matches without any very high runs. As I mentioned, I know a man who won a major 14.1 tournament championship with a high run of only 54.

You are improving very well if, after six months of play, you can run 15 balls in a row. Actually, that's a terrific accomplishment. If you can make 15 it means you can conceivably run 30 or 45.

A more important indication of your progress, though, is in pocketing the ball. If you can make a difficult shot, there's hope for you. Above all, if you've got a feel for the game and you really like it, you'll develop into a good player.

Banks and Caroms

As a beginner, you're going to find it's hard enough to make a ball go straight. So don't go after a carom shot, where you ricochet the cue ball off one object ball and into another, or a bank shot, where you drive the object ball into one or more cushions before pocketing it.

These shots are flashy and challenging, but very, very difficult. So wait until you're an advanced player before attempting them.

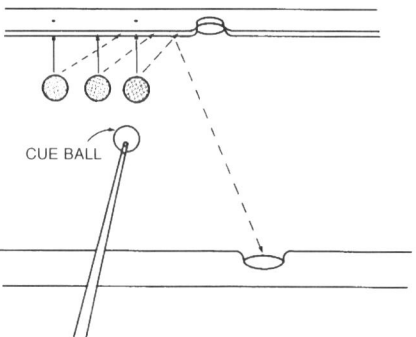

Figure 3.9 A BANK SHOT. When banking a ball, estimate the space between the ball and the pocket nearest to it. Bisect the angle, and try to hit the ball to a point that is halfway between the ball and the pocket.

Bank shots are tough because of the difficulty you have in judging the angle at which the object ball is going to leave the cushion. Often the angle will increase as the speed of the object ball decreases.

There are different types of carom shots. The most common is the one in which you carom the cue ball off a first object ball and into a second with the second object ball pocketed. In another shot, you carom one object ball off a second and the first object ball then proceeds to the pocket.

You'll have to carom or bank, for example, when you're *snookered*—when there are one or more balls between the cue ball and the object ball you want to pocket.

A kiss, as a carom is sometimes called, may be a desirable smack on the lips, but in pocket billiards, where it refers to one ball glancing

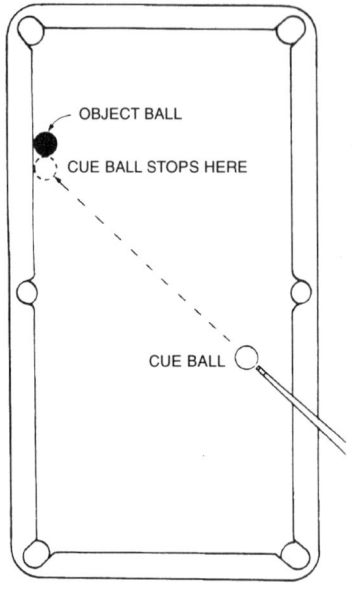

Figure 3.10 When the object ball is frozen to a cushion, strike the cue ball so that it hits the cushion and the object ball simultaneously.

off another, it's not always pleasurable. Sometimes you'll want a ball to kiss another for purposes of position and you'll shoot for it to happen. But at other times a kiss will occur by accident and the balls may become frozen—touching a rail or one another—in a way that creates problems for you on your succeeding shots.

Combinations

A *combination shot* involves driving your cue ball into one or more object balls, which in turn strike the object ball you're trying to pocket. It's another temptation that, for the most part, you ought to resist.

Unless you know that the combination is lined up absolutely straight for the hole, don't shoot for it. In fact, if there's any doubt at all about the combination, go to your alternative shot. And if you have a straight-in shot, by all means take that one first.

There may be times, such as when you're trying to break up a cluster, that you have no alternative but to try a combination. In that case, pay particular attention to the ball that will be hit right before the one you're trying to pocket. That ball is the key in determining whether you can pocket the one you want to. That ball will tell you whether it's possible to make the shot at a proper angle.

4
The Games People Play

There are innumerable games other than eight ball that you can play on a pool table, all of them fun and all of them requiring combinations of the skills and strategies dealt with in previous chapters.

On the following pages are several—but by no means all—of the popular games that players have found exciting and challenging over the years. There's nothing to prevent you from taking elements of some of them and combining them into original games of your own. Please note: many of the games are played with variations of the rules given here.

There should be enough games here to keep you happy at the billiards table for a long time. For all of the rules and specifics, see the official rule book of the Billiard Congress of America.

14.1

The game that used to be played in billiard championships was *14.1 continuous pocket billiards*, a form of straight pool that requires all-around playing skill. If you learn to play 14.1, you'll be able to play any pocket billiard game, so let's talk about playing strategy, special situations, and pitfalls.

The object of 14.1 is to score a specific, predetermined number of points before your opponent does. In friendly games, you can set any point total as the winning score—say 50 or 100 points. In championship play, 150 is the customary total. The game is sometimes known as *call shot*, because in order to score, you've got to designate the object ball at which you're aiming and the pocket into which you intend to drop it. You get one point for every ball you hit into a designated pocket. You also get a point for any ball pocketed along with a legal shot. The game is played with a cue ball and 15 object balls numbered from 1-15. In 14.1, each ball is worth a point.

At the start of the game, the cue ball is in hand—that is, placed anywhere between the head string and the head of the table—and the numbered balls are set in a triangle at the foot of the table. The 15-ball is placed on the foot spot at the head of the triangle, the 1-ball goes at the rear right corner, and the 5-ball is placed at the rear left corner. The player who opens drives the cue ball into one or more of the balls in the rack.

Key Ball and Break Ball

What makes the game of 14.1 continuous is that after 14 of the object balls have been pocketed, the 15th ball stays on the table as the *break ball*. The 14 pocketed balls are then racked up and the game continues.

Your chances of running up a high score or running out—winning the game—depend on whether or not you can keep going through the transition from one or two balls left on the table to when they're re-racked and all 15 balls are in play.

The key to how well you're progressing in pool often lies in how you handle the *key ball*, the next-to-last ball on the table before you re-rack.

A good player will decide when several balls are left which one will be the key shot and will maneuver accordingly. If you're capable of making the decision, pocketing the key shot, and getting into excellent position for the break shot, you're on your way to becoming a good player.

Which ball is your break ball is usually fairly obvious. For one thing, you'll want it to be one that is relatively close to where the triangle of balls will come, because, as you know, the farther your cue ball has to travel, the tougher the shot will be.

Continue making the ball outside the triangle. Your strategy is to pocket the break ball in a pocket that you call and have the cue ball carom from the break ball into the triangle of racked balls. You can also carom the cue ball from the break ball into one or more cushions and then into the rack.

You don't have to shoot at the break ball. You continue until you miss or scratch, or until you score the required number of points for the game.

If the last ball on the table is left within the perimeter of the triangle where the other balls are to be racked, that ball is spotted on the head spot. If the cue ball and unpocketed object ball interfere with the racking of the 14 balls, all 15 object balls are re-racked. If the cue ball interferes with the racking of the balls, one of two things happen: if the break ball is outside of the head string, the cue ball is in hand and you can place it anywhere behind the head string for the break. If the break ball is within the head string (in the area between the head string and the head of the table), the cue ball is placed on the head spot. If the break ball happens to be there, it is moved to the center spot to allow the cue ball to be placed on the head spot.

Whatever the situation, if you decide to shoot into the rack rather than at the break ball, you've got to either pocket a ball, drive an object ball to a cushion, or make the cue ball hit a cushion after contacting an object ball.

Penalties

There are some things to watch for in 14.1. One of them is making sure that when you play safety with an object ball that's frozen against a cushion, you either pocket the object ball, make the cue ball contact a cushion after it strikes the object ball, or drive the object ball to another cushion. Otherwise, you lose a point.

Even if you don't violate this rule, you can play safety in this situation only twice in succession. On the third shot, you must either drive the object ball to a different rail or drive the cue ball to any rail after it makes contact with the object ball. Failure to do so will mean that all 15 balls are racked, and that you'll have to break as you would at the beginning of the game.

When the cue ball is in contact with an object ball, you may play directly at that object ball, but you must move the object ball and cause the cue ball to strike a cushion or drive that object ball to a cushion. If you don't do one of these, you lose a point.

When you foul and have no points to your credit, your score becomes minus-1, minus-2, or however many points you owe. When you count, what you owe is deducted from your score.

As mentioned earlier, three scratches in succession cost you a 15-point penalty in addition to one point off for each scratch. To add insult to injury, you then have to break open 15 balls as at the beginning of the game.

A ball that goes into a pocket and bounces out doesn't count as pocketed. If a cue ball jumps off the table, it counts as a foul, with loss of point and turn. If an object ball goes off the table, it just ends the inning. The ball is spotted.

If the cue ball jumps up accidentally as a result of a legal stroke, or deliberately, by the player's elevating the butt end of the cue and striking the ball in the center or above center, it's a legal jump. But if you dig under the cue ball with the tip, causing the ball to jump, you lose a point.

BASIC POCKET BILLIARDS

Object

The game of *basic pocket billiards* involves only one rack of balls, and the first player or team to pocket eight balls wins the game.

The Break

In basic pocket billiards, players lag, choose, or draw lots for the opening break. The break is done with cue ball in hand. The player who breaks must either pocket a ball or drive two object balls in addition to the cue ball to a cushion. If your opponent breaks and fails to do this, you get the cue ball in hand. You can place the cue ball anywhere within the head string.

Rules

In most respects, basic pocket billiards is played like 14.1, but there are some differences. After the opening shot, you have to call the ball or balls you intend to pocket, but you don't have to designate the pocket at which you're aiming. On the opening shot, you get credit for any balls pocketed; you don't have to call them.

Later, if you call more than one ball, you have to pocket all the balls you called, or none will count. If you miss a called ball, but the cue ball touches any object ball it's not an error. Like 14.1, basic pocket billiards involves continuous play.

Penalties

In basic pocket billiards, penalties consist of forfeiting one ball and point, plus any balls pocketed on the foul stroke.

A player loses a point each time he or she fails to comply with break shot requirements. Other grounds for penalties include scratching the cue ball in a pocket, forcing the cue ball off the table, shooting while the balls are in motion, striking the cue ball twice on the same stroke, touching a ball with the cue in any way except on a legal stroke, or failing, after the opening stroke, to pocket a ball, to cause an object ball to hit a cushion, or to cause the cue ball to hit a cushion after striking the object ball.

Playing Strategy/Winning Tips

Because only eight balls wins this game, it's important to avoid scratching and imperative that you don't leave your opponent an easy shot that can start him on a winning run.

FIFTEEN-BALL POCKET BILLIARDS

Object

The object of this game, which is played with a cue ball and 15 object balls, is to be the first to score 61 points. The numbers on the object balls total 120 points, and you get the number of points on the ball that you pocket. For example, the 7-ball is worth 7 points.

The Break
The balls are racked up in a triangle, the 15-ball at the foot spot. The next high-numbered balls are placed near the 15-ball. On the opening break, you must either pocket a ball or drive at least two object balls to a cushion. You don't have to call your shots, either on the break or on subsequent play. If you fail to break properly, your opponent has the option of requiring you to break again.

Rules
After the opening stroke of the game, if you don't pocket a ball you must either drive an object ball to a cushion or make the cue ball hit a cushion after it makes contact with an object ball.

All balls made on one legal stroke are credited to the player who pockets them.

If the game ends in a tie, you can either play the whole game over or spot the 15-ball on the foot spot, lag for the next shot, and reopen play with the cue ball in hand. Whoever scores the 15-ball wins.

Penalties
Penalties are costly in this game: you lose three points each time you fail to comply with the requirements of the opening break shot. You also lose three points if the cue ball is pocketed, if a ball is not pocketed and you fail either to drive an object ball to a cushion or to make the cue ball go into a rail after it hits an object ball, if you hit the cue ball off the table, if you shoot out of turn, if you hit a ball when it's in motion, and if you fail to have one foot on the floor when you're stroking. If you commit more that one foul simultaneously, you lose only three points.

Playing Strategy/Winning Tips
It obviously pays in this game to go after the high-numbered balls. But a word of caution: don't take a nearly impossible shot at say, the 14-ball, and run the risk of ending your inning when you've got a safer shot at a 6-ball or 7-ball. Take the shots you can make.

ROTATION

Object
One of the old standbys of the pool table is *rotation*, which is also called sixty-one because scoring 61 points clinches the game. You get points according to the number on the ball you pocket—one point for the 1-ball, two points for the 2-ball, and so on. This game is like fifteen-ball pocket billiards, with one major exception: in rotation, after the opening break, you have to

Figure 4.1 The balls as they are racked for rotation.

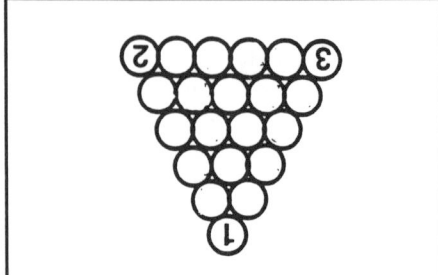

pocket the balls in rotation, starting with the 1-ball and working up.

The Break

The balls are racked up with the 1-ball in front and the 2-ball and 3-ball in the left and right rear corners of the triangle, respectively. The rest of the balls are racked at random.

Players lag, choose, or draw lots for the break. If you're the one who breaks, you must make the 1-ball your first object ball. If you fail to contact the 1-ball first on the break shot, your inning ends. Any other balls pocketed on the shot are spotted. Your opponent accepts the ball in position and makes the 1-ball his first object.

If you do make contact with the 1-ball on the break, you get credit for any other balls that are pocketed. So on the break, while aiming at the 1-ball, try to break all balls wide open.

Rules

After the 1-ball is pocketed, the 2-ball becomes the legal object ball, then the 3-ball, and so forth. The lowest-numbered ball on the table is always the object ball. The cue ball must strike the legal object ball before making contact with any other ball, or your inning ends. As long as you first make contact with the legal object ball, you're entitled to all balls pocketed on the shot, whether or not you pocket the legal object ball.

By the way, there is no scratch in rotation. If the cue ball should go in the pocket, there is no point penalty. But it is the end of your inning.

Balls illegally pocketed are spotted on the long string, the imaginary line that runs from the foot spot to the center of the foot rail. Balls are spotted in numerical order. For example, if the 1-ball and 3-ball are illegally pocketed, the 1-ball is placed on the foot spot and the 3-ball

Figure 4.2 Spotting balls.

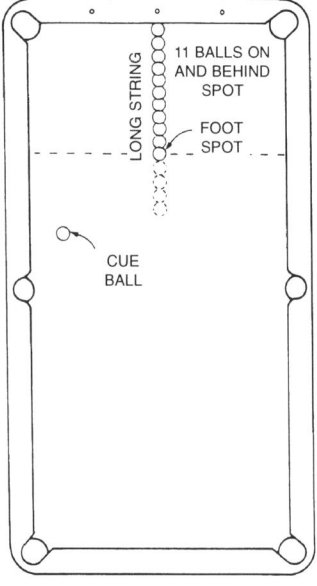

is frozen right behind it on the string. If the foot spot is occupied, the spotted balls are placed as close as possible to the spot, in numerical order. Never move the cue ball or an object ball that happens to be on the long string to make room for a ball to be spotted. Instead, place the spotted balls either in front or behind those object balls on the long string. If the cue ball is on the long string so that it interferes with spotting of an object ball, the object ball is placed in front or behind the cue ball as close to the foot spot as possible.

If the entire long string is occupied, the balls to be spotted are placed in front of the foot spot and as close to it as possible.

If an object ball jumps the table, it is spotted. If you cause one or more object balls to jump the table but you made contact with the legal object ball first, you are credited with any object balls you pocketed on the stroke. If you fail to score, your inning ends.

If the cue ball jumps the table, it's an error and ends your inning. Any balls pocketed on that stroke are spotted, and your opponent continues with cue ball in hand.

If the legal object ball lies between the head string and the head of the table, and you've got cue ball in hand, the legal object ball is placed on the foot spot.

Playing Strategy/Winning Tips

The rules of rotation prescribe the strategy you must employ. You've got to make sure that you hit the legal object ball first. This is a game where you may be forced into a carom shot because your object ball may be hidden by other balls. If this happens, proceed with the utmost care and caution. Figure 4.3 shows how I would handle a typical playing situation.

Among veteran players, games played at a pool table are divided into categories—"money games," "gentlemen's games," and "girl-friend games."

The two games preferred for wagering are *nine ball* and *one*

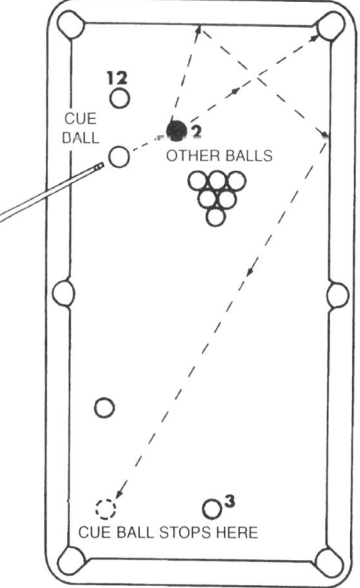

Figure 4.3 The 12-ball is an easy shot, but the game of rotation requires that the 3-ball be made after the 2-ball, a very difficult shot. I would use a hard follow with right-hand English to pocket the 2-ball and get into position for the 3-ball.

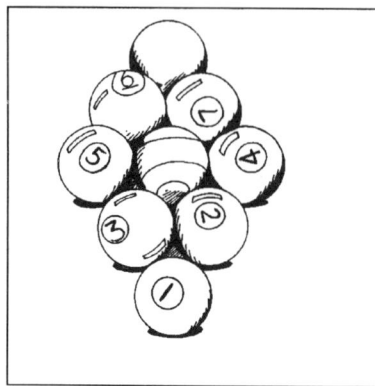

Figure 4.4 The balls as they are racked for nine ball.

pocket. The reason these are the favorites of money players is that they're finished quickly, and hustlers like to win or lose their money fast. You can enjoy playing these games whether or not you gamble on them.

NINE BALL

Object

In pool, the biggest money game by far is *nine ball,* whose object, as you can tell from the name, is to sink the 9-ball.

The Break

For this game the balls are racked with the 1-ball at the head and the 9-ball in the middle. The other balls are placed at random.

Rules

The strategy in nine ball is to break the balls wide open and to try to sink any one of them. Then, beginning with the 1-ball, you try to sink the balls in numerical order until you sink the 9-ball. You can play a combination involving the 9-ball, just as long as you also hit the ball you're aiming at. If you should hit the 1-ball and that hits the 9-ball and they both go in, you win. You need a good bit of luck. You don't have to call your shots.

Playing Strategy/Winning Tips

This is one game in which it's advantageous to break, because you might make a ball and continue until you run out. You might even make the 9-ball on the break. When I break in nine ball, I place the cue ball almost in the middle of the table, just 2 or 3 inches off the head spot, and aim for the center of the cue ball, driving it right at the middle of the 1-ball. I hit it as hard as I can and hope.

The one thing you have to be careful of is scratching, even though it won't cost you a point. You can't let your cue ball go into the pocket or your turn ends and your opponent will probably run the table.

ONE POCKET

Object

In *one pocket,* you and your opponent each select a pocket as your own before the game begins. Most likely, you'll pick one of the pockets at the foot of the table, since that's where balls are likely to go on the break. The object of the game is to sink eight balls in your pocket. The first player to do so wins the game.

Rules
Balls do not have to be played in rotation or in any specific order, and you don't have to call the balls you're trying to sink. Just make eight of them in your pocket.

Playing Strategy/Winning Tips
This is a game where defensive play is critical and the mental aspect is strong. It's like a chess game in that you're thinking four or five moves ahead and, even as you're moving offensively, you're playing defense. Try to leave your opponent the hardest bank possible. Don't take gambles, because in the long run you'll lose out.

Let's say we lag and I break. Since you seldom are able to make a ball in your pocket on the break, I would hit what's called a safe break—a very easy hit to protect myself. I'll try to get as many balls as possible near my pocket, without leaving you a clear shot at yours. If I'm successful, it puts you on the defensive. You have to get the balls that are near my pocket out of there because if you don't, I'll probably sink two or three more. So you have to protect yourself at all times. If you make a tactical mistake, you'll have to be very lucky to get away with it.

Carom or bank shots are an important part of this game since, if your opponent is skillful, you're not going to be left with any straight-on shots. But caroms take a lot of skill and I don't recommend them until your game is well-developed.

GOLF POCKET BILLIARDS

A game that borrows from a different pastime is *golf pocket billiards*.

Object
The object of this game is to play six holes in the fewest possible strokes.

The Break
You use only a white cue ball and any one object ball. To start, place the cue ball on the center spot and the object ball on the foot spot. If you're the starting player, you have to bank the object ball against the foot cushion on the first stroke, as you attempt to pocket the ball in the left side pocket.

Figure 4.5 The balls set up for golf pocket billiards.

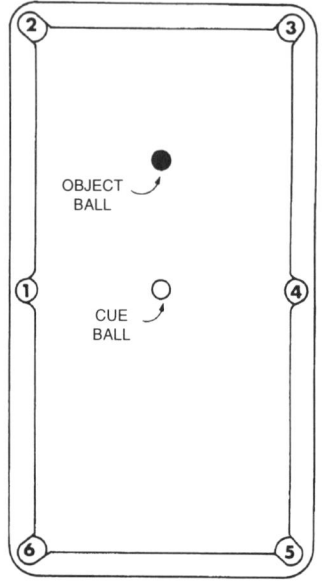

Rules

If you miss the bank shot on the first stroke, you continue to shoot until you pocket the ball, shooting either directly at the object ball or banking it, as you see fit. After that first stroke, you're not compelled to bank. When you finally pocket the ball in the left side pocket, you add up the strokes it took you and keep that as your score for the first hole.

Now it's your opponent's turn. Again the balls are spotted—the cue ball on the center spot and the object ball on the foot spot. Your opponent, too, must bank to the lower rail on the first stroke, as he or she tries to pocket the ball in the left side pocket. Your opponent's score for the first hole is totaled.

It's your turn again. The object ball is spotted on the foot spot once more, but the cue ball is left where it was when your opponent scored his or her opening shot. This time, you're aiming to pocket the ball in the upper left hand corner hole. You don't have to bank this shot, although you can. Keep stroking until you sink the ball.

The object ball is spotted once more, the cue ball is left where it was when you pocketed the ball, and your opponent now tries to make the ball in the upper left corner hole in as few shots as possible.

After that, keep alternating as you aim for the upper right-hand side pocket, the lower-right-hand corner pocket, and, finally the lower-left-hand corner pocket—in that order. Each player has an inning at each hole. The one who completes the six holes in the fewest number of strokes wins the game.

Partners

If you should play the game with partners, as many players like to do, the partners' scores are added together, and the team with the lowest number of strokes wins.

In partners, if you take the opening stroke and miss, your partner then attempts to pocket the ball, and you keep alternating until the ball is dropped into the designated hole. If you should make the ball on the first shot, your partner will lead off the next inning.

On a change of turn, the only time the object ball is not spotted is when the object ball lies within the head string.

Penalties
Scratches occur in golf pocket billiards when you pocket the cue ball or when you sink the object ball in the wrong pocket. The penalty adds three strokes to your score, plus the one stroke for the shot. If you should double-scratch—pocket the object ball in the wrong hole and also pocket the cue ball—you're assessed only one penalty. The scratched balls are spotted and you continue playing. This is different from most other pocket billiard games, where you lose your turn when you fail to pocket a ball.

On every shot the object ball either has to be pocketed or hit a cushion or the cue ball has to hit a cushion after it strikes the object ball. If you fail to do any of these things, it will cost you three extra strokes in addition to one for your shot. Play continues with the balls left where they are.

CRIBBAGE POCKET BILLIARDS

Object
The object of *cribbage pocket billiards* is to score more cribbages than your opponent. To score a cribbage—or one point—you've got to pocket two balls whose point value totals 15 (say the 6-ball and 9-ball, or the 3-ball and 12-ball) in the same inning. The 15-ball counts as a cribbage itself, but that must be left for last.

The Break
This game is played with the cue ball and 15 numbered balls. You start cribbage pocket billiards in the same way as you do 14.1, with the balls racked in a triangle at the foot spot in no particular numerical order.

If you open, you don't have to call your break shot, but, as in 14.1, you've got to drive two or more object balls as well as the cue ball to a cushion, or pocket an object ball. If you fail to comply with these regulations, you lose a point and can be compelled to break again. If you miss the second time, your opponent accepts the balls in position.

Rules
It doesn't count to pocket more than two balls that add up to 15 (say the 4-ball, 5-ball, and 6-ball). That would be an error and end your inning.

The 15-ball must be left for last. If you score a cribbage legally (two balls totaling 15 in the same inning), your turn continues, and you can try for another in the same inning. If you should make, say, the 3-ball, but miss the 12-ball, the 3-ball is spotted.

Whoever has the most cribbages when all balls are pocketed wins the game.

Playing Strategy/Winning Tips
If you don't have relatively easy shots at one or both of the balls you need for a particular cribbage, play for safety.

FORTY-ONE POCKET BILLIARDS

Object
This is a game in which an exact score is necessary to win. Your aim is to score 41 points, which is a combination of the point value of the balls you pocket plus a private number that you're given. You must keep the number from your opponents until you're ready to declare that you've got 41.

The Break
The game is played with a cue ball and 15 object balls, plus a leather shaker bottle containing small balls or "peas," or pieces of paper with numbers on them, usually numbered from 1 to 15. Rotation of play is determined by throwing each player a small ball from the bottle. The player with the lowest number has to break. Before play starts, each player is thrown another numbered ball from the bottle for his private number.

Rules
Once you've pocketed the number of points that, when added to your private number totals 41, you announce it and show your private number.

One rule that's very different about this game is that whether or not you pocket any balls, you're allowed just one shot per inning. If you should pocket more than one ball on a single stroke in an inning, you get credited for them all.

If all the balls should be pocketed before anyone has 41, the player whose count is closest to 41 wins. If you play safety, you have to make the cue ball hit a cushion before or after contacting an object ball. Otherwise, you scratch and owe a ball.

Bursting
If you should get more than 41 points, that's a *burst* and you must declare it or be disqualified from continuing in the game. If you want, you can get a new private number and begin again.

Penalties
If you miss or pocket the cue ball, you've scratched, and you owe a ball to the table, plus balls you may have scored on the shot. If you have more than

one ball to your credit, you can spot any ball you choose. If you owe a ball and you've got none in your rack, you have to spot the first ball you legally count. If you score more than one when you owe one to the table, again you may choose which one to spot.

When you burst and all your balls are spotted, the last ball pocketed has to be placed on the foot spot or as near as possible behind it.

ONE-AND-NINE BALL

One-and-nine ball is a four-handed game, with the partners selected after the game has started.

The team that scores 61 points first wins the game. Balls are valued according to their face numbers.

The Break
Balls are racked as in the game of rotation, with the 1-ball on the foot spot at the apex of the triangle and the 2-ball and 3-ball in the left and right rear corners, respectively.

Rules
Played with a white cue ball and 15 numbered object balls, the game uses the rules of 14.1 and rotation pocket billiards.

The balls must be pocketed in rotation. The player who scores the 1-ball automatically becomes the partner of the player who pockets the 9-ball. If it turns out that the same player pockets both the 1- and 9-balls, he or she becomes the partner of the player who scores the 10-ball. If the 10-ball is off the table, the one who pockets the 11-ball is his or her partner.

It's possible that each side may have 60 points when all the balls are pocketed. If so, the player who pocketed the last ball places that ball on the foot spot and has the cue ball in hand within the head string. He continues his inning. Play continues until one side or the other pockets the lone ball on the table.

5
What Makes a Good Player

Earlier we talked about the equipment you need to play pocket billiards, but we didn't mention the most important factors of all—the physical and mental qualities that ultimately determine how good a player you can be.

To be a player of championship calibre, you must either be born with a special talent or else start playing when you are an infant and keep at it throughout your life. Whether or not you have that natural something it takes to be a champion, you can still develop into a very good player, regardless of the age at which you start, your sex, size, build, or strength—provided you have a few things going for you to start with and you're willing to work hard.

Basically, you need three qualities to be a competent pool player: good coordination, good eyesight, and the right mental attitude.

If you're a born klutz, you probably won't ever be a champion, but you can develop your condition to the top limits of your natural ability through practice. Playing the game is the best means.

Eyesight is naturally an important factor in playing pool, simply because you have to see where you're hitting the ball. I happen to be nearsighted and wear glasses, but I don't wear them when I'm playing. Through some kind of happy turn of fate, I can see the length of the table without special lenses. I can hit a ball as thin as I want, breeze it, or just rock it back and forth, if I want to.

The better your eyesight, the more finely you'll be able to cut a ball. But even if your eyesight is poor, or if you wear glasses, you can still learn to play well. Just compensate by concentrating on position play so that you won't have to cut the ball as precisely in order to pocket it. In other words, the easier the angle of the shot you leave yourself, the less squinting and precision-shooting you'll need to make a ball.

Generally speaking, pool is a game of areas—you'll seldom hit the ball to the exact point you're aiming at every time. If you can hit the ball to the general area of the pocket, you will, if all goes well, make the shot.

MENTAL ATTITUDE

One of the biggest factors in how well you play pocket billiards is mental attitude. If you don't have the desire to excel, you'll never be more than a fair player, if that. If you don't have the will to win and the ability to play under pressure, you're not going to play well, and you certainly can't be considered championship calibre, although even at the top ranks there are some players who choke when the going gets rough. The ability to play under fire is pretty much an inborn quality—either you have it or you don't—but there are outside factors that can influence you and your mental condition.

If you're pressured by your job or financial burdens, you're usually not going to do well in game competition. You have to be relaxed and well-rested, with your mind at ease. When you get out there at the table, your mind must be only on what you're doing. You have to block out everything else—the crowd, your opponent's reputation, the argument you had at home or at work—and concentrate totally on your game. The key word is concentrate, whether you're playing for money or for fun, whether you're in a championship match in front of a crowd or relaxing in a friendly game in your own basement.

There will be situations when you've got to be willing to take risks in the game, without getting wild, in order to win. If, for instance, there's a trouble ball that should be pocketed at once, and you don't have the courage to try the shot, it could mean that you might as well put up your hands and surrender because your opponent is probably going to start a run that wins the game. If you are willing to take the chance, though, you've got to be cool enough to give yourself the best possible chance of making the ball. Pool is 80 percent skill and 20 percent luck. If you can play under pressure, you've got a much better chance that your luck will be good.

CONFIDENCE

A significant part of proper mental conditioning is self-confidence. If you don't have the confidence that you're going to succeed in life, you're probably going to wind up a failure. It's also true of pocket billiards. You've got to believe you can do it. Wanting to is the first step.

It's good to be confident, but you should guard against overconfidence. It can cost you points and games.

Don't let up. Always play as hard as you can, until the last ball is pocketed. When I think I've got an easy match, or when I'm way ahead, I tend to slacken. The fact is that I play better when I'm behind. Maybe it's peculiar, but those are the times when I have more of a competitive edge.

Overconfidence sometimes shows when you start taking too much for granted. You think you can make any shot on the table, and so you go in and shoot wildly. That's a form of overconfidence to avoid. The game looks easy, but it isn't, as you'll be reminded if you don't keep your confidence under control.

PHYSICAL CONDITION

Mental condition is all-important, but don't overlook your physical condition. You play best when you're in the best of health, so try to avoid illness and get as much rest as possible. Don't expect to play well when you've been drinking, and try to stay clear of smoke-filled rooms that will cause eye irritation.

Unlike a lot of other sports, pocket billiards can be played, and played well, by physically handicapped persons. I've known physically challenged people, including a man who lost a leg in combat, who aren't hindered by their handicaps when it comes to playing pool.

DRESS COMFORTABLY

Until you get into the World Championships or the U.S. Open, there's no reason for you to dress in anything but what you find most comfortable. There's no regulation uniform. Loose-fitting clothes are the best, because they don't interfere with the fluid motion of your stroke.

PSYCHING

In a game where fractions of an inch can spell victory or defeat, it helps to have nerves of steel. Some players are easily rattled, and some have calm temperaments. Try your best not to let anything disturb you.

Maybe it's because I started playing exhibitions so young, but I'm a player who has a reputation for being able to take almost any distraction in stride.

If somebody at one of the tables makes a great shot just as you're about to shoot, you should have enough savvy to stand up, walk away from the table, and take a drink of water.

As cool as I am, I'm constantly rubbing the tip of my cue stick with a dollar bill or sandpaper (which, as I mentioned earlier, you shouldn't use anywhere on your shaft). Somehow, it relaxes me and gives me confidence to know that my tip has the right smoothness. Another thing that relaxes me before a match is powdering my hands. You'll find your own little habits that serve to calm you. Don't worry about them, if they do the job.

Whether or not it helps, some players will resort to all kinds of measures to throw your game off. I had one opponent who went to the bathroom seven times during one rack of balls. It was deliberate, I'm sure, but he wasn't penalized for delaying the game. That's something that's up to the referee's discretion.

The professional referees who oversee professional matches are the sole judges. You can't argue with their decisions and expect to change anything.

Another "sharking" tactic is to casually wave a handkerchief around the eye level of a player, hoping he'll start paying attention to the handkerchief instead of his game.

AMBIDEXTERITY

There are good reasons for you to experiment playing both right-handed and left-handed, mainly because conditions will arise on the table where it's difficult to make a shot with your usual power hand.

But don't start fooling with your second hand until you've become pretty good with your first.

I was originally right-handed, but my father, a professional baseball player (and a pretty fair pool player), wanted me to become a left-handed pitcher, and he switched me when I was about four years old. I've been left-handed ever since, but I've always been able to do certain things right-handed. I can play golf from either side, and throw a baseball, bat, or bowl with either hand. I can play pool with either hand. I'm more proficient left-handed, so in a tournament I'll shoot with that hand with one exception: when it's a choice of shooting with my right or using the mechanical bridge, I'll shoot right.

INDEX

[Note: Bold page numbers denote illustrations.]

Aiming and sighting the ball, 22-23, **22**
Ambidexterity, 58

Balls, 1-2
Basic pocket billiards, 43-44
Bridge(s)
    hand, 11-12, **12, 13,** 14, **15, 16,** 17, **17, 18,** 19
    mechanical, 6, **6,** 19-20, **19, 20**
    rail, 14, **15, 16,** 17, **17, 18,** 19
    shooting over a ball, 14

Chalk, 7-8, **7**
Clothing, 57
Confidence, 56-57
Coordination, 55
Cribbage pocket billiards, 51-52
Cue stick(s)
    caring for a, 5-6
    choosing a, 4-5
    described, 2-3
    sections of, 3-4, **4**

Draw shots, 26-27, **26**

Eight ball
    break, 31
    object, 31
    rules, 31-32
    strategy/tips, 32-34, **35,** 36-40, **36, 38, 39, 40**
English, 27-28, **28, 30**
    curve, 30
    natural, 28, **29**
    reverse, 28, **29**
Eyesight, 55

Fifteen-ball pocket billiards, 44-45
Follow shots, 26, **26**
Forty-one pocket billiards, 52-53
14.1 continuous pocket billiards, 41-43

Golf pocket billiards, 49-51, **50**
Grip, 20, **21,** 22

Mental attitude, 56-58

Nine ball, 48, **48**

One-and-nine ball, 53
One pocket, 48-49

Physical condition, 57
Powder, 8
Psyching, 57-58

Rotation
    break, 46, **46**
    object, 45-46
    rules, 46-47, **46**
    strategy/tips, 47-48, **47**

Stance, 9, 10, 11
Stroke(s)
    aiming and sighting the ball, 22-23, **22**
    curve, 30
    draw shots, 26-27, **26**
    English, 27-28, **28, 29,** 30, **30**
    follow shots, 26, **26**
    follow-through, 25
    sticking the cue ball, 27
    warmup, 24-25

Table, 1, **2**
Triangle, 7

The Winning Edge of Sports Series

Billiards for Advanced Players
by STEVE MIZERAK
With Joel Cohen

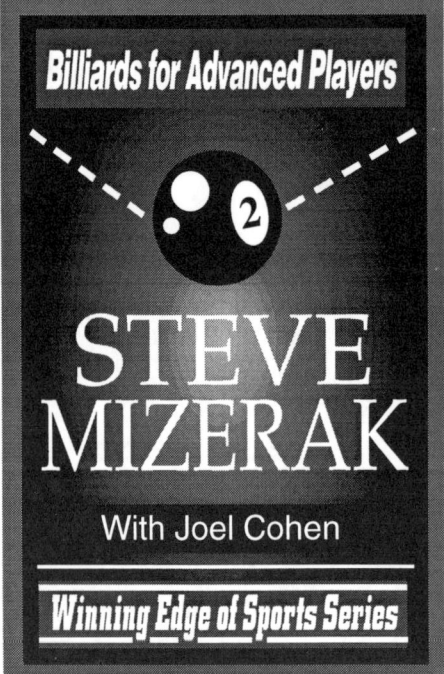

This book will make you a better shot and will give you a rudimentary understanding of the strategies involved in good tavern pool. What makes a good player? Practice! But for further instruction everyone should take professional instruction, seek out video tapes and reach for a more advanced book. A synergistic instructional program will win tournaments.

Here are a few of Steve Mizerak designed products you will find in bookstores, billiards dealers, pool halls and sports shops near you. Ask for them by name. For a dealer near you call 800/541-7323

$12.95 in U.S.A.
$17.95 in Canada
ISBN 1-57034-045-5

Watch and Learn from the Masters

Three Masters of the game show you, how to play pool with the best of them. Learn it all, every detail–shot by shot, game after game. **Pocket Billiards,** *Fundamentals to Fantasticks* with Steve Mizerak, Ewa Mataya and Johnny Archer. and **POOL,** *The Masters Way* with Steve Mizerak, Pretty Boy Floyd and Ewa Mataya.
Both Tapes $19.95 plus $5.00 shipping.
Call 1-407-840-0048